# The Macintosh
# Digital Hub

by Jim Heid

Peachpit
Press

Avondale
MEDIA

**The Macintosh Digital Hub**
Jim Heid

**Peachpit Press**
1249 Eighth Street
Berkeley, CA 94710
510/524-2178
510/524-2221 (fax)
Find us on the World Wide Web at: www.peachpit.com
To report errors, please send a note to errata@peachpit.com

Peachpit Press is a division of Pearson Education
Copyright © 2003 by Jim Heid
Editor: Barbara Assadi, BayCreative
Art Direction/Illustration: Arne Hurty, BayCreative
Compositors: Jonathan Woolson, Sarah Ewalt
Production Coordinator: Lisa Brazieal
Copyeditor: Kelly Anton
Technical Editor: Victor Gavenda
Indexer: Emily Glossbrenner, FireCrystal Communications
Cover design: Doug Beach, afstudio

ISBN 0-321-12529-0
9 8 7 6 5 4 3
Printed and bound in the United States of America

*For Maryellen,*
*for my mother,*
*and in loving memory*
*of George Heid, my dad.*
*A master of the analog*
*hub, he would have*
*loved this stuff.*

George Heid (right),
recording direct to disc
on a moving train,
in the early 1950s.

# Acknowledgements

The Macintosh Digital Hub is the result of the heroic efforts of an exceptional group of people, all of whom have my thanks and admiration.

One of them also has my love. My deepest thanks go to Maryellen Kelly, my wife, colleague, and best friend. It's been 20 years now, and it's more fun than ever. I adore you.

Next up are the dream teams that helped produce the DVD and book. On the book front, there's the dynamic duo of Barbara Assadi and Arne Hurty, principals of San Francisco's BayCreative. Their company name should be WayCreative, because they are. Arne's design and illustration talents grace the book and DVD, while Barbara expertly polished the prose and managed a project whose schedule defied the space-time continuum. It was a joy working with you both again.

In the production trenches, Jonathan Woolson dug himself in and didn't leave until the layouts glittered, making insightful design and content recommendations all the while. And Sarah Ewalt came through to produce the iMovie section just as our deadline clock approached midnight. Kelly Anton gave the copy a final read and made sure all the i's were dotted and the t's were crossed.

Thanks also go to everyone at Peachpit Press: to Marjorie Baer and Nancy Ruenzel, for having the vision to recognize just how slick this project could be; to Lisa Brazieal, for deftly handling its production requirements; to Victor Gavenda, for going over the DVD with a fine-toothed comb; and to Scott Cowlin and Kim Lombardi, for spreading the word.

Then there's the other dream team. The DVD wouldn't have happened without Steve Broback and Toby Malina, my partners at Avondale Media and my good friends. A spin of the Avondale disc also goes to Bethany Mitchell, Joan Hudson, and Brett Davis. And the video owes its look to the talents of Eric Stromberger, director of photography and master of lighting; B. T. Corwin, the artist behind the lens; Tom Wolsky, production consultant and Final Cut Pro master (your book rules!); Paul Anderson, technical consultant and fun dinner companion (your next Kincaid is on me!); and Vicky Helstrom, makeup artist.

And finally, the last-but-definitely-not-least department: thanks to Terry Oyama for the beautiful Once Upon a Dream; to Laura Ingram; to Alicia Awbrey and Keri Walker; to Rennie and everyone at MCN; to Bob Laughton and my KZYX friends; to the Mendocino Cookie Company (don't forget the extra foam); and to Trixie, who's sweeter than any cookie.

Jim Heid

# Table of

v   Acknowledgements

viii   DVD Table of Contents

x   Read Me First:
Using the Book and DVD

## Touring the Digital Hub

2   Personal Computers
Get Personal

4   A Sampling of the
Possibilities

6   Where the Mac Fits In

8   Putting the Pieces
Together

10   Essential Add-Ons:
Outfitting Your Mac
for Digital Media

## iTunes and iPod: Making Music

14   iTunes at a Glance

16   Importing Music from CDs

18   Customizing Importing
Settings

20   A Matter of Perception:
How MP3 Works

22   Tags and More:
MP3 Nuts and Bolts

24   Sequencing Songs
with Playlists

26   Playlist Tips

28   Find that Tune:
Searching and Browsing

30   Improving Sound
Quality with the Equalizer

32   Burning CDs

34   Tuning In to
Internet Radio

36   Internet Radio:
The Rest of the Story

38   Analog to Digital: Converting
Tapes and Albums

40   iTunes Tips

42   Adding On:
Scripts and Beyond

44   iPod: Music to Go

46   Setting iPod Preferences

48   iPod Tips

50   iPod as Address Book
and More

## iPhoto: Organizing and Sharing Images

54   iPhoto at a Glance

56   The Essentials of
Digital Imaging

58   Importing Photos
into iPhoto

# Contents

60 After the Import: Getting Organized

62 Assigning and Editing Keywords

64 Creating Albums

66 Editing Photos

68 Using the Edit Window

70 Searching for Photos

72 Sharing Photos on a HomePage

74 More Internet Sharing Options

76 Printing Photos and Ordering Prints

78 Creating Books

80 Creating Slide Shows

82 More Ways to Share Photos

84 iPhoto Tips

86 More iPhoto Tips

88 Tips for Better Digital Photography

## iMovie: Editing Video

92 iMovie at a Glance

94 Importing Video

96 Importing Other Assets

98 Working with Clips

100 Timeline Techniques: Adding Clips to a Movie

102 Editing Techniques and Tips

104 Audio Insights: Working with Sound

106 Adding Transitions

108 Creating Titles and Effects

110 It's a Wrap: Exporting to Tape

112 Other Export Options

114 iMovie Tips

116 Tips For Making Better Movies

## iDVD: Putting it All Together

120 iDVD at a Glance

122 Adding Movies and Slide Shows

124 Customizing Your DVD's Interface

126 Menu and Interface Design Tips

128 Burning Your DVD

130 iDVD Tips

132 More iDVD Tips

135 Index

The Macinosh Digital Hub

DVD

Table of Contents

1   Introduction

2   iTunes and iPod:
    Making Music

3   Importing Tracks
    from a CD

4   Creating Playlists

5   Opening a Playlist in a Window

6   Making a Playlist from a
    Selection

7   Searching for Songs

8   Sorting and Adjusting Columns

9   Browsing Your Song Library

10  Controlling iTunes While
    You Work

11  Using the Equalizer

12  Burning an Audio CD

13  Labeling a CD

14  Automating iTunes with
    AppleScripts

15  The G-Force Visualizer

16  Adding Speakers

17  Apple's iPod

18  Setting iPod Preferences

19  A Case for the iPod

20  Playing the iPod Through
    a Stereo

21  Noise-Canceling Headphones

22 iPhoto: Organizing and Sharing Photos

23 Touring the iPhoto Window

24 Importing Photos from a Camera

25 Importing Photos from the Finder

26 Rotating Vertically Oriented Photos

27 Creating Albums

28 Viewing and Modifying an Album

29 Assigning Titles to Photos

30 Deleting Photos from an Album

31 Editing and Cropping a Photo

32 Using the Image-Editing Window

33 Creating a Slide Show

34 The iTools Music Library

35 Creating a HomePage

36 Ordering Prints

37 Printing Within iPhoto

38 Printing With Portraits and Prints

39 FireWire Media Reader

40 Dedicated Photo Printer

41 Creating a Book

42 Thinking Beyond Paper

43 iMovie: Making Movies

44 Importing Video from a Camera

45 Importing Media

46 Copying Images from iPhoto

47 Copying an MP3 from iTunes

48 Importing Media into iMovie

49 Naming Clips

50 Making a Montage

51 Creating Soundtrack Markers

52 Cropping and Adding Clips

53 Using the Undo Command

54 Playing a Movie Back

55 Creating an Audio Bed

56 Adjusting the Volume of a Clip

57 Adding a Transition

58 Taking Out the Trash

59 Adding Still Images to the Timeline

60 Adding Another Audio Bed

61 Tweaking the Soundtrack

62 Zooming the Timeline

63 Mixing Audio Track Levels

64 Adding a Title

65 Refining the Audio Track

66 Replacing the Music Track

67 Exporting to a Camera

68 Connecting a TV Set

69 Adding a FireWire Hard Drive

70 Adding a FireWire Hub

71 iDVD: Putting it All Together

72 Theme Park: Touring iDVD

73 Customizing a Theme

74 Removing the Watermark

75 Changing the Title Design

76 Staying in the TV-Safe Area

77 Exporting a Movie for iDVD

78 Adding a Movie and Customizing its Button

79 Creating a Slide Show

80 Adding Photos from iPhoto

81 Adding a Soundtrack from iTunes

82 Previewing the Slide Show

83 Adding Audio to a Menu

84 Turning Off a Motion Button

85 Burning a DVD

86 Wrapping Up

87 Credits

# Read Me First: Using the Book and DVD

Why combine a book and a DVD? Because each has its own strengths. The printed word conveys depth and detail, but many people learn best by watching over someone's shoulder. Video lets you see for yourself, and video on a DVD lets you watch in any order you want.

Print and video complement each other, and that's why you will find references to the DVD throughout this book. It's also why many DVD segments point you to the book.

Where should you begin? You decide. If you're new to the digital hub, you might want to break open a Mountain Dew and watch the DVD from start to finish. Or, watch the introduction, then use the DVD's main menu to jump to the segment you're most interested in. Or, keep the book near your Mac as a reference, and check out chapters of the DVD when you want to see something in action.

How you master the digital hub is up to you; just have fun doing it.

## How the Book Works

This book devotes a separate section to each spoke of the digital hub: iTunes and iPod for music; iPhoto for photography; iMovie for video editing; and iDVD for creating DVD-Video discs. Each section is a series of two-page spreads, and each spread is a self-contained reference that covers one topic.

Most spreads begin with an introduction that sets the stage with an overview of the topic.

Most spreads refer you to relevant chapters on the DVD to help you locate video that relates to the current topic.

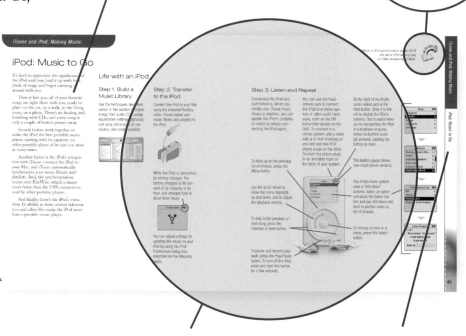

The book and the DVD assume you're using Mac OS X, although much of the iTunes and iMovie material also applies to the Mac OS 9 versions of these programs.

Here's the main course of each spread, where you'll find instructions, background information, and tips.

The section and spread names appear on the edges of the pages to allow you to quickly flip to specific topics.

# How the DVD Works

*The Macintosh Digital Hub* DVD plays on any standard DVD player, as well as on Macs (and PCs) equipped with DVD drives. Because of the nature of video, picture quality is a bit better if you play the DVD on a TV set instead of on your computer. Still, you may find it fun to have the DVD playing in a small window on your computer monitor as you learn about a digital hub program.

To return to the Main Menu, press your DVD remote's Title key (which may instead be called Top Menu or Disc).

To watch a segment, choose its menu item. When that segment ends, playback continues on to the next segment. Use your DVD player's Menu button to return to the main menu.

Most DVD player remote controls have number keypads. You can jump straight to a topic by pressing its number. See your DVD player's user manual for details on entering numbers using your remote control.

To browse the DVD by topic, choose Jump to Topic. To return to the topic menu, press your DVD remote's Menu key.

When you choose a segment from this menu, you see another menu that lists the topics within that segment.

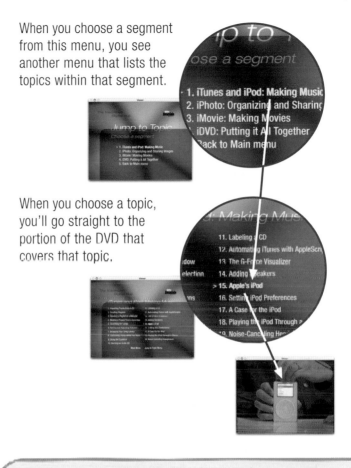

When you choose a topic, you'll go straight to the portion of the DVD that covers that topic.

## Jumping to Specific DVD Chapters

*The Macintosh Digital Hub* DVD contains 87 chapters; their numbers appear in the DVD Table of Contents and in the Go To DVD references throughout the book. You can use your DVD player's search feature to enter those chapter numbers and jump to a specific spot. See your player's instructions to learn how to use its search functions.

If you're viewing the DVD on your Mac, you can also use the Mac OS X DVD Player program to quickly access a chapter. Choose Go To Chapter from the Script menu (the little scroll-shaped menu to the left of the Help menu), and then double-click on the chapter you want to view.

# Touring the Digital Hub

## The Macintosh Digital Hub

# Personal Computers Get Personal

Music, photographs, and movies can inspire, amuse, persuade, and entertain. They're time machines that recall people and places. They're vehicles that carry messages into the future. They're ingrained in infancy and become intensely personal parts of our lives. And they've all gone digital.

It's now possible to carry a music library in your pocket, to take photos without film, and to edit video in your den—or on a cross-country flight. It's easier than ever to combine music, images, and video. And it's easy to share your finished product, whether with loved ones in the living room, clients in a conference room, or a global audience on the Internet.

Behind this digital age are breakthroughs in storage technologies, processor speed, chip design, and even in the types of connectors and interfaces used to attach external gear. In the past, personal computers weren't powerful enough to manage the billions of bits that make up digital media. Today, they are.

You might say that personal computers have finally become powerful enough to become truly personal.

## Audio

| 1962 | 1972 | 1979 | 1982 | 1988 |
|------|------|------|------|------|
| Bell System begins first digital phone transmissions. | Nippon Columbia Company begins digitally recording master tapes. | Sony's Walkman is the first portable music player. | Billy Joel's 52nd Street is the first album released on CD. | CDs outsell vinyl albums for the first time. |

## Imaging

| 1969 | 1986 | 1991 | 1992 |
|------|------|------|------|
| Bell Labs researchers invent the charge-coupled device (CCD). | Kodak develops first megapixel CCD. | Kodak adapts Nikon F-3 camera with 1.3-megapixel CCD. | Kodak's Photo-CD system puts scanned images on CDs. |

## Video

| 1956 | 1967 | 1975 | 1983 | 1985 |
|------|------|------|------|------|
| First videotaped TV program is broadcast. | Sony delivers first portable videotape recorder. | Bell Labs demonstrates CCD TV camera. Sony Betamax debuts. | Sony's Beta-movie is the first one-piece camcorder. | Small, 8 mm tape cassettes allow for compact camcorders. |

## Storage

| 1956 | 1973 | 1980 |
|------|------|------|
| IBM disk system holds 5 megabytes and uses disks two feet wide. | First hard disk: 30MB on an 8-inch disk platter. | Philips and Sony develop the compact disc standard. |

**1989**
German research institute Fraunhofer patents MP3 audio compression.

**1990**
Digital audio tape (DAT) recorders debut.

**1991**
Sony's Mini-Disc format debuts.

**1996**
Fraunhofer releases MP3 encoder and player for Windows PCs.

**1999**
Napster and other Internet services enable swapping of MP3 files.

**2001**
Apple introduces iPod. First copy-protected audio CDs appear amid controversy.

**2002**
Apple updates the iPod with a 10GB hard drive.

## Truly Personal Computing

**1994**
Apple's Quick-Take 100 camera debuts at $699.

**1997**
The Associated Press switches to digital photography

**1998**
1-megapixel cameras proliferate. Online photo sites offer prints and other services.

**1999**
2-megapixel cameras, led by Nikon's $999 Coolpix 950, are the rage.

**2000**
3-megapixel cameras add movie modes. Digital cameras represent 18 percent of camera sales.

**2001**
Consumer cameras hit 4 megapixels. Digital cameras comprise 21 percent of camera market.

**2002**
Apple introduces iPhoto.

**1987**
New digital video formats are used by broadcasters.

**1989**
Hi-8 format brings improved image and sound quality.

**1991**
Apple's Quick-Time 1.0 brings digital video to the Mac.

**1994**
miniDV format debuts: digital audio and video on 6.3 mm-wide tape.

**1995**
FireWire, invented by Apple in the early 90s, is adopted as industry standard.

**1999**
Apple builds FireWire into Macs and releases iMovie 1.0.

**2001**
Apple wins Primetime Emmy Engineering Award for FireWire.

**1984**
First Mac hard disks store 5MB and cost over $2500.

**1992**
Apple includes CD-ROM drives with Macs.

**1993**
A 1.4GB hard drive costs $4559.

**1995**
DVD standard is announced.

**1999**
IBM's MicroDrive puts 340MB on a coin-sized platter.

**2001**
5GB Toshiba hard drive uses 1.8-inch platter; Apple builds into iPod.

**2001**
Apple builds DVD burners into Macs

# A Sampling of the Possibilities

This technological march of progress is exciting because it enables us to do new things with age-old media. I've already hinted at some of them: carrying a music library with you on a portable player, shooting photographs with a digital camera, and editing digital movies.

But the digital age isn't about simply replacing vinyl records, Instamatic cameras, and Super 8 movies. What makes digital technology significant is that it enables you to combine various media into messages that are uniquely yours. You can tell stories, sell products, educate, or entertain.

And when you combine these various elements, the whole becomes greater than the sum of its parts.

## Sell a Product

Create a DVD whose video and images allow prospective customers to see your product in action.

## Bring Back the Past

Relive a memorable vacation with digital images, video, and sounds.

## Create for the Future

Produce a book of photographs that commemorates a baby's first year.

## Tell a Story

Interview relatives and create a
multimedia family history, complete with
old photographs and oral histories.

## Have Fun

Put your favorite photo on a mousepad, a
coffee mug, a T-shirt—or a dozen cookies.

## Tunes on the Road

Carry your music with you, and plug your portable
player into a stereo system when you get there.
Or use an adapter to listen on your car radio.

## Become a Digital DJ

Create playlists that play back your favorite
tunes in any order you like.

## Educate

Create a training video that teaches
a new skill—or a new language.

## Promote Yourself

Distribute a portfolio of your design
work or photography on a DVD.

# Where the Mac Fits In

All of today's personal computers have fast processors, fat hard drives, and the other trappings of power. But powerful hardware is only a foundation. Software is what turns that box of chips into a jukebox, a digital darkroom, and a movie studio.

Software is what really makes the Macintosh digital hub go around. Each of Apple's digital hub programs—iTunes for music, iPhoto for photography, iMovie for video editing, and iDVD for creating DVDs—greatly simplifies working with and combining digital media.

Equivalent programs are available for PCs running Microsoft Windows. But they aren't included with every PC, and they lack the design elegance and simplicity of Apple's offerings. It's simple: Apple's "iWare" has made the Mac the best personal computer for digital media.

Of course, hardware *has* helped.

### iMovie
- Capture video from camcorders
- Edit video and create titles and effects
- Add music soundtracks from iTunes
- Save finished video to tape or disk

### iDVD
- Create slideshows from iPhoto images
- Add music soundtracks from iTunes
- Present video created in iMovie

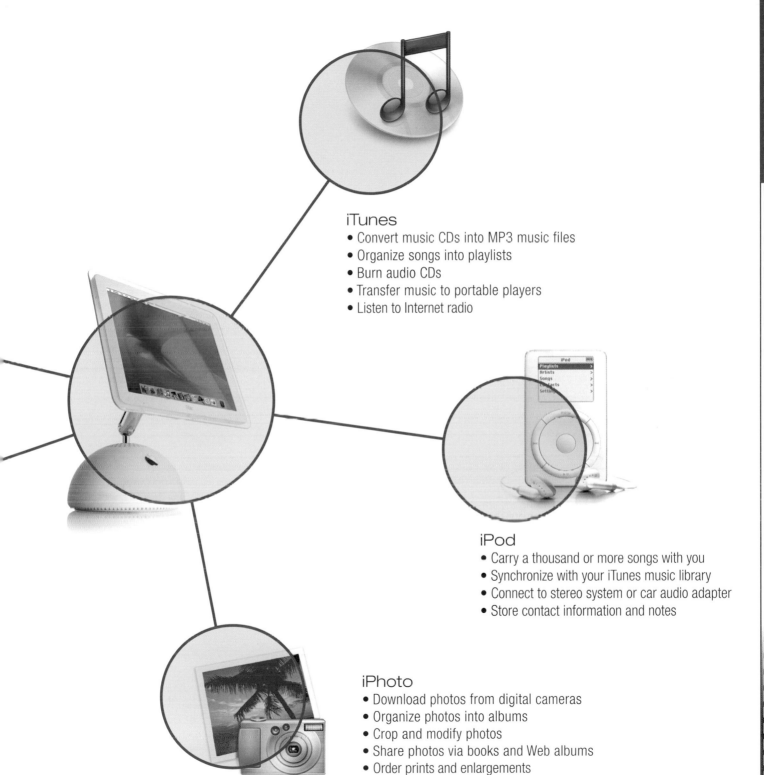

## iTunes
- Convert music CDs into MP3 music files
- Organize songs into playlists
- Burn audio CDs
- Transfer music to portable players
- Listen to Internet radio

## iPod
- Carry a thousand or more songs with you
- Synchronize with your iTunes music library
- Connect to stereo system or car audio adapter
- Store contact information and notes

## iPhoto
- Download photos from digital cameras
- Organize photos into albums
- Crop and modify photos
- Share photos via books and Web albums
- Order prints and enlargements

# Putting the Pieces Together

Several aspects of the Mac's hardware make it ideally suited to digital media work. One is the speed of the PowerPC, the central processor at the heart of each Mac.

Converting audio CD tracks into MP3 music files, generating special video effects, preparing video for burning onto a DVD—these are demanding tasks, far more demanding than moving words around, calculating budget spreadsheets, or displaying Web pages. But the PowerPC G4 chip contained in most Macs has special circuitry—Apple calls it the Velocity Engine—which specializes in performing complex calculations.

Another factor in the hardware equation is ports: the connection schemes used to attach external devices, such as portable music players, digital cameras, camcorders, printers, and speakers. Every Mac contains all the ports necessary for connecting these and other add-ons.

And finally, the Mac's hardware and software work together smoothly and reliably. This lets you concentrate on your creations, not on your connections.

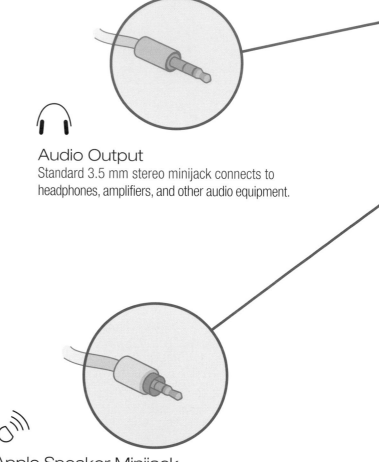

## Audio Output
Standard 3.5 mm stereo minijack connects to headphones, amplifiers, and other audio equipment.

## Apple Speaker Minijack
Connects to Apple Pro Speakers. This special jack has a smaller diameter (2.5 mm) than the headphone jack so that you can't inadvertently plug headphones into it.

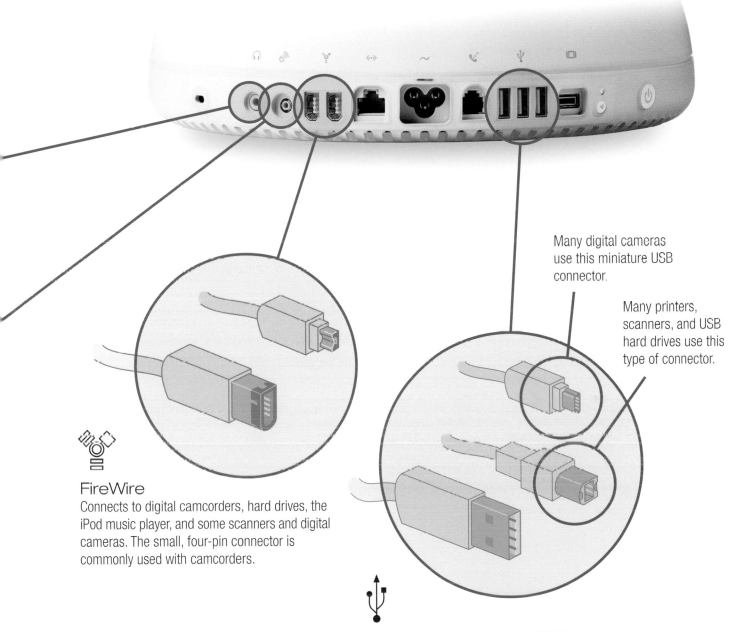

### FireWire
Connects to digital camcorders, hard drives, the iPod music player, and some scanners and digital cameras. The small, four-pin connector is commonly used with camcorders.

Many digital cameras use this miniature USB connector.

Many printers, scanners, and USB hard drives use this type of connector.

### Universal Serial Bus (USB)
Connects to digital cameras, scanners, some speaker systems, microphones, printers, and other add-ons.

# Essential Add-Ons: Outfitting Your Mac for Digital Media

With their built-in USB and FireWire ports, today's Macs are well equipped to connect to cameras, portable music players, camcorders, and other digital devices.

But there's always room for improvement. To get the most out of Apple's iWare, consider upgrading several key components of your Mac. Here's a shopping list.

## Memory

Adding memory is a great way to boost any Mac's overall performance. And with most Macs, you can install a memory upgrade yourself. (With older iMac models that have tray-loading CD-ROM drives, it's a good idea to have memory installed by a qualified technician.)

Add as much memory as you can afford. I consider 384 megabytes (MB) to be a bare minimum for digital hub work; 512MB or more are better.

## Hard drive

All digital media eat up a lot of disk space—except for video, which utterly devours it. If you're serious about digital hub work, you'll want to expand your Mac's storage.

It's easy to do. If you have a tower-style Mac, you can install a second hard drive inside the Mac's case. For iMacs and PowerBooks, you can connect an external FireWire hard drive—or several of them, if you like.

External FireWire hard drives are available in a wide range of capacities and case sizes. Portable drives are particularly convenient: they fit in a shirt pocket and can draw power from a Mac's FireWire jack—no separate power supply needed. On the downside, though, portable drives cost more than conventional external drives.

## Speakers

Some Mac models include the Apple Pro Speakers, lovely transparent orbs that sound surprisingly rich for their small size.

You can also buy the Apple Pro Speakers separately, but note that they require a Mac containing a special jack. They work with flat-panel iMacs and newer Power Mac models, but not with Power Macs introduced prior to 2001.

See a portable FireWire hard drive, WiebeTech's fast and rugged MicroGB, in the iMovie segment of the DVD.
○ **69**

See the Apple Pro Speakers and other audio add-ons in the iTunes segment of the DVD.
○ **16-21**

The small size of the Apple Pro Speakers means their bass response is a bit anemic. To beef up your bass, consider adding Harmon Kardon's iSub. This subwoofer connects via USB and sits under your desk, although its exotic, jellyfish-like design will tempt you to keep it out where everyone can see it. And its deep, gut-punching bass will amaze everyone who hears it.

If you don't yet have a speaker system, Harmon Kardon's SoundSticks system is a great choice. It includes an iSub-like subwoofer and two see-through acrylic satellite speakers that sit on either side of the Mac.

One drawback to all the speakers I've discussed here is that they can't connect to an iPod or other device that uses a standard stereo miniplug. The Apple Pro Speakers use an oddball connector, and the iSub and SoundSticks connect via USB.

If you'd like a more versatile set of speakers—ones that will connect to virtually any audio device—go for a system such as JBL's Sonnet, which provides a standard stereo miniplug and includes a subwoofer and two satellite speakers. Or connect your Mac or iPod to a stereo system, either directly or through an FM transmitter, as shown on the DVD.

## A FireWire hub

See two FireWire hubs in the iMovie segment of the DVD.
🔘 70

The Mac's FireWire connectors are durable, but they aren't indestructible. All that plugging and unplugging of camcorders, hard drives, iPods, and other doodads can take its toll. What's more, many Macs have just one FireWire connector, limiting the number of devices you can connect directly to the Mac.

A FireWire hub is an inexpensive add-on that addresses both issues. A hub is to FireWire what a power strip is to a wall outlet: it provides more jacks for your devices. After connecting the hub to your Mac, you can connect several devices to the hub.

You can also buy USB hubs that provide the same expansion benefits for USB devices.

## An iTools account

Okay, so this isn't an add-on per se, but it is something you'll want. If you sign up for a free Apple iTools account, you'll be able to create your own Web page and Web photo albums using iPhoto. You'll also be able to access Apple's iDisk remote storage service, where you'll find lots of software downloads as well as a library of royalty-free music that you can use in your digital hub endeavors.

To sign up for iTools, go to www.apple.com and click the iTools button. Note that by signing up, you're giving Apple permission to send you advertising via email and postal mail. If you don't want that, be sure to uncheck the Stay Informed box in the iTools sign-up screen.

# iTunes and iPod: Making Music

## The Macintosh Digital Hub

# iTunes at a Glance

All media may have gone digital, but music was there first. In the 1980s, the compact disc format turned the clicks and pops of vinyl into relics of the past—at least until hip-hop music brought them back.

More recently, the grassroots groundswell behind the MP3 format led to a frenzy of Internet music swapping and CD burning. And the trend continues to keep recording industry executives awake at night and put food on the table for more than a few lawyers.

MP3 and other digital audio formats have created a new era of musical freedom. Not freedom to steal—copying an artist's efforts without paying for them is just plain wrong—but freedom to arrange songs in whatever order you like and to play those songs on a variety of devices.

iTunes is the program that brings this freedom of music to the Mac. With iTunes, you can create MP3 files from your favorite audio CDs, and then organize those MP3 files into playlists. You can listen to your playlists on a Mac, burn them onto CDs, or transfer them to an iPod portable music player.

The arrow buttons skip to the previous or next song in a playlist. To skip forward and backward within a playing song, click on an arrow and hold down the mouse button.

Play/Pause (keyboard shortcut: spacebar).

Adjusts the volume.

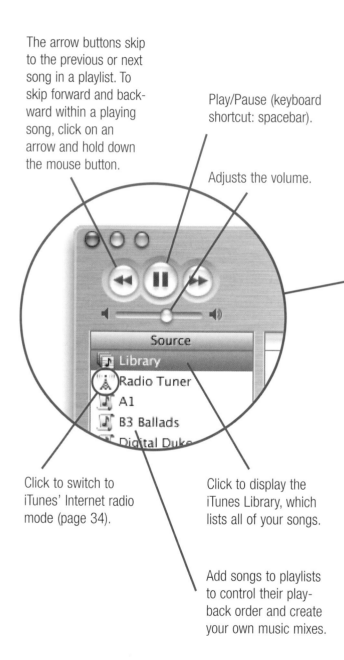

Click to switch to iTunes' Internet radio mode (page 34).

Click to display the iTunes Library, which lists all of your songs.

Add songs to playlists to control their playback order and create your own music mixes.

See and hear iTunes and
some software and
hardware add-ons 💿 2.

Click this tiny button to switch between song information and iTunes' animated spectrum display.

Click the time display and artist name to view other time options and album information.

Drag the diamond left or right to scan through a song.

To sort a list by a specific column, click that column's heading. To reverse the sort order, click the heading again. To resize columns, drag their left and right boundaries.

Use the Browse button to view your music by artist and album (page 28).

Use the Search box to quickly locate songs (page 28).

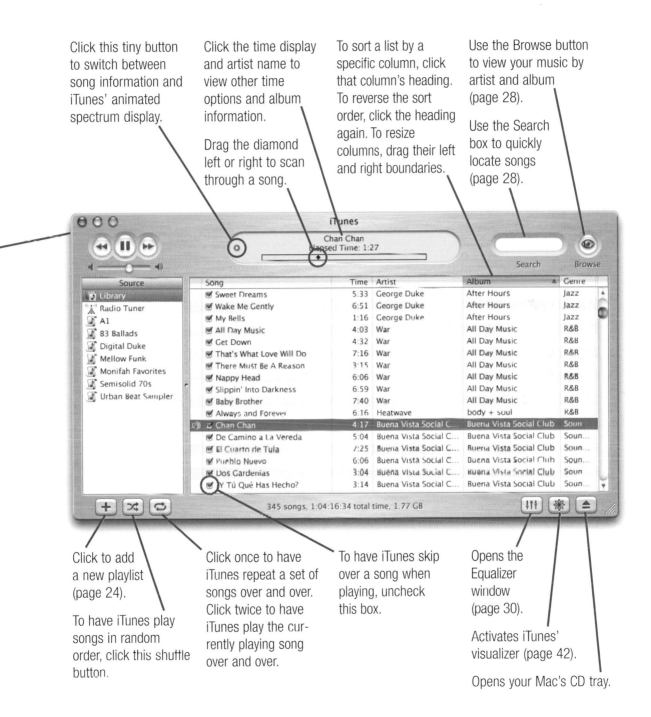

Click to add a new playlist (page 24).

To have iTunes play songs in random order, click this shuffle button.

Click once to have iTunes repeat a set of songs over and over. Click twice to have iTunes play the currently playing song over and over.

To have iTunes skip over a song when playing, uncheck this box.

Opens the Equalizer window (page 30).

Activates iTunes' visualizer (page 42).

Opens your Mac's CD tray.

15

# Importing Music from CDs

The first step in stocking your digital jukebox involves bringing in music from your audio CDs. Apple calls this process *importing*, but most MP3 fans refer to it as *ripping* (from the Latin, meaning "to rip off").

Whatever you call it, iTunes is good at it. Insert a compact disc into your Mac's CD drive, and iTunes launches, connects to the Internet, and retrieves the name of the CD and its tracks. Click iTunes' Import button, and the program converts the CD's contents into MP3 files that are stored on your Mac's hard drive.

That's the big picture. You can create a vast digital music library with iTunes without having to know any more than that. But iTunes has several features that give you more control over the ripping process. You can, for example, specify that iTunes import only certain songs. And as described in later sections, you can customize the MP3 compression settings that iTunes applies to the music it imports.

Just want to play a CD instead of ripping it? Click the play button or double-click on any track.

Rips all tracks with check marks before their names.

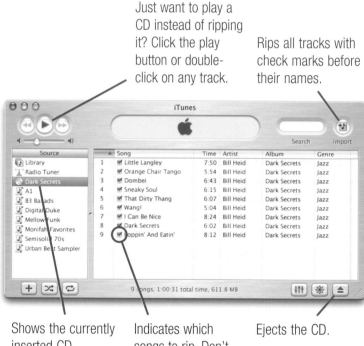

Shows the currently inserted CD.

Indicates which songs to rip. Don't like some songs? Uncheck their boxes, and iTunes will not import them.

**Tip:** To uncheck all tracks, press ⌘ while clicking on a track's check box.

Ejects the CD.

# How iTunes Retrieves Track Names

Back in the late 1970s, when the compact disc standard was being developed, no one foresaw the digital hub era. As a result, the developers of the CD standard didn't create a way for CDs to store artist, album, and track names.

So how can iTunes retrieve this information? The answer lies in the fact that no two audio CDs are the exact same length. A CD is comprised of a specific number of blocks, each of which is one seventy-fifth of a second long. You might say that

every CD has its own unique digital fingerprint.

In 1996, some clever programmers in Berkeley, California, realized they could create a database that would link these fingerprints to specific information. The compact disc database, or CDDB, was born. Soon, CDDB spawned a company, Gracenote,

which provides disc-lookup features to Apple and other companies that have MP3- and music-related products.

When you insert a CD, iTunes calculates its digital fingerprint and then sends it over the Internet to Gracenote's server. If Gracenote finds a match, it transmits the corresponding information back to iTunes, which displays it.

# Power Ripping: Changing CD Insert Preferences

Doing some binge ripping? Save yourself time and set up iTunes to automatically begin importing as soon as you insert a CD. Choose Preferences from the iTunes menu, then check the setting of the On CD Insert pop-up menu. Choose Import Songs or, better yet, Import Songs and Eject.

# Customizing Importing Settings

CD-quality stereo sound requires about 10MB of disk space per minute. By using *compression*, MP3 can lower audio's appetite for storage by a factor of 10 or more. (To understand how this loss of appetite occurs, see "A Matter of Perception: How MP3 Works" on page 20.)

MP3 sound quality depends in large part on how much the audio has been compressed. Compression is measured in terms of *bit rate*—the average number of bits required for one second of sound. To obtain near CD-quality audio, MP3 requires a bit rate in the range of 128 to 192 kbps (kilobits) per second. Higher bit rates mean less compression and better sound quality.

But the higher the bit rate, the larger the file. In this era of huge hard drives, file size may not be as important to you as sound quality. But if you're trying to shoehorn a vast music library onto a portable player—or if your hard drive is nearly full—you may need to assess how much space your MP3s are using.

iTunes is set up to encode at 160 kbps, striking a good balance between file size and sound quality. You can change those settings by choosing Preferences from the iTunes menu, and then clicking the Importing tab.

You don't have to fuss with iTunes' encoding settings at all, but if you're an audiophile or you're just curious, go ahead and experiment: rip a few songs using various settings, and then compare their file sizes and audio quality.

If you don't want to compress your music at all, choose the AIFF or WAV encoders, and iTunes will make exact copies of the tracks on the CD. But note that those tracks will require 10MB of disk space per minute. (AIFF, which stands for Audio Interchange File Format, is a standard audio format on the Mac; WAV is its equivalent on Windows. Both formats are broadly supported on Macs and Windows.)

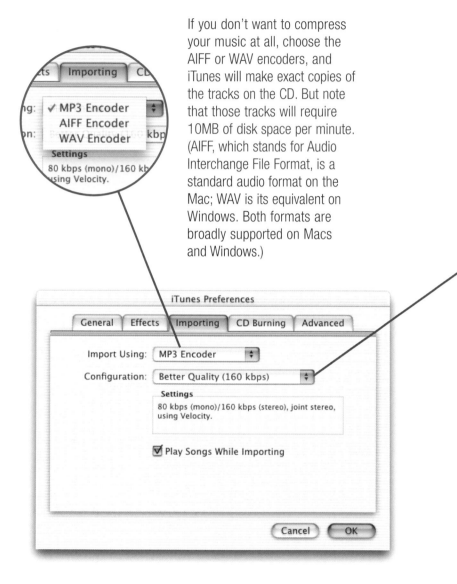

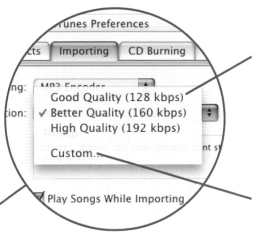

128 kbps is closer to FM-radio quality than to CD quality—you may notice a swirling quality to instruments that produce high frequencies, such as strings and cymbals. 192 kbps delivers better quality than 160 kbps, though my ears have trouble detecting it.

To explore the kinds of adjustments MP3 allows for, choose Custom to display the dialog box shown below. See below for custom setting choices.

Tweaks your encoding settings for the best quality given the bit rate settings you've specified. You can usually leave this box checked, but if you're a control freak who doesn't want iTunes making adjustments for you, uncheck it.

Specify the desired bit rate here. Monophonic audio requires a lower bit rate than does stereo, since there's only one channel to encode.

Variable bit rate (VBR) encoding varies a song's bit rate according to the complexity of the sound. For example, a quiet passage with a narrow range of frequencies is less "demanding" than a loud passage with a broad range of frequencies. VBR uses disk space more efficiently and, according to many MP3 fans, sounds better, too. Many iTunes users turn on VBR and then lower the bit rate—for example, encoding at 128 kbps with VBR instead of at 160 kbps without VBR.

iTunes will filter out inaudible, low frequencies. Leave this one checked.

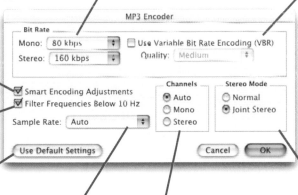

Click to restore iTunes' original settings.

Leave this pop-up menu set to Auto for most uses. If you're encoding a voice recording, however, you can save disk space by lowering the sample rate to 22.050 KHz or even 11.025 KHz.

In the Auto setting, iTunes detects whether the original recording is in stereo or mono. To force iTunes to encode in mono—for example, to save disk space—click Mono.

Our ears have trouble discerning where high frequencies are coming from. Joint Stereo encoding exploits this phenomenon by combining high frequencies into a single channel, saving disk space. Careful listeners say they can sometimes hear a difference in the spatial qualities of a recording.

# A Matter of Perception: How MP3 Works

You don't have to understand how MP3 works in order to use iTunes, but you might wonder how an MP3 file can be roughly one-tenth the size of an uncompressed audio file and still sound nearly the same.

MP3's origins go back to the 1980s, when researchers began exploring ways to reduce the storage requirements of digital audio. One of the standards that came from these efforts was MPEG (Moving Picture Experts Group) Audio Layer III—MP3 for short.

Like many audio compression schemes, MP3 relies heavily on *perceptual encoding*, which eliminates those portions of an audio signal our ears don't hear well anyway. It's similar to how the JPEG image format works, compressing images by throwing away image data our eyes don't detect easily. Because some information is lost in the process, MP3 and JPEG are called *lossy* compression schemes.

MP3 is not the only audio compression scheme, nor is it the best. Compression technologies developed for streaming Internet audio are much more efficient than MP3—they require lower bit rates to achieve the same levels of quality.

MP3's dominance, then, comes not from technical superiority, but from its grassroots popularity and the wide availability of MP3 software and music files.

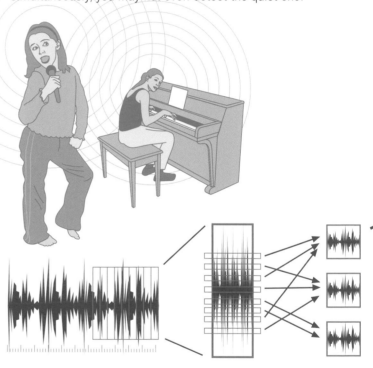

The uncompressed audio on a CD contains more information than our ears can detect. For example, if a loud sound and a quiet one reach your ears simultaneously, you may not even detect the quiet one.

An MP3 encoder's first step is to break the original audio into a series of *frames*, each a fraction of a second in length.

The encoder further breaks down each frame into *sub-bands* in order to determine how bits will need to be allocated to best represent the audio signal.

The encoder compares the sub-bands to *psychoacoustics tables*, which mathematically describe the characteristics of human hearing. This comparison process, along with the bit rate that you've chosen for encoding, determines what portion of the original audio signal will be cut and what portion will survive.

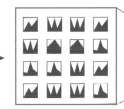

**Example:** A faint squeak produced by the foot pedal of a drum is cut because it happens at the same instant that a cymbal is struck.

Finally, the encoded data is further compressed by about 20 percent using *Huffman* compression, which replaces redundant pieces of data with shorter codes. You do the same thing every time you say "a dozen eggs" instead of saying "egg" twelve times.

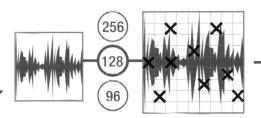

| 6 of | 2 of |
| 4 of | 6 of |

# Where iTunes Stores Your Tunes

You'll want to back up your music library now and then to avoid losing it to a hard drive failure or other problem. But where is the library? In your Documents folder.

Inside the Documents folder is another folder named iTunes. Inside that folder are two items: a folder named iTunes Music and a file named iTunes Music Library (2).

**iTunes Music Library (2)**

The iTunes Music Library (2) file contains a database of all the songs you've added to iTunes, as well as all the playlists you've created. But it doesn't contain the MP3 files themselves. Those files live in the iTunes Music folder.

Note that you don't have to store MP3s that you rip in the iTunes Music folder. If you'd like to store them elsewhere—on a portable FireWire hard drive, perhaps, or maybe on a file server, where everyone on a

To tell iTunes where to store MP3s that you rip, click Change.

home network can access them—choose Preferences from the iTunes menu, click the Advanced tab, and then specify the desired location.

It's also worth noting that you can have MP3 files scattered all

over your hard drive if you like—or even on multiple hard drives. For more details, see "Adding MP3s from Other Sources" on page 40.

# Tags and More: MP3 Nuts and Bolts

Here's another section you're welcome to skip if you're just getting started with MP3 and iTunes. But if you do skip it, I guarantee you'll be back. Why? Because there will be times when you'll want to edit the information for a song that iTunes displays.

Maybe the song is from an obscure CD that isn't in Gracenote's CDDB, and iTunes has given its tracks generic names like *Track 5*. (This will also happen if you rip a CD when not connected to the Internet.) Or maybe CDDB stored the song names in all-lowercase or all-capital letters, and you'd like to correct that.

Or maybe you've encountered a problem similar to the one illustrated at right. I ripped two CDs from jazz piano giant, Bill Evans. For one of the CDs, CDDB retrieved the artist name as *Bill Evans*, but for the other CD, it retrieved the name as *Bill Evans Trio*. When I transfer those songs to my iPod, I have two separate listings in the Artist view—even though both listings refer to the same artist.

For situations like these, you can use iTunes' Get Info command to edit the information of one or more songs. First, select the song whose attributes you want to edit, and then choose Get Info from the File menu, or press ⌘-I.

Specify the song's name as you'd like it to appear in iTunes and on a portable player.

iTunes displays size, date, format, and location information here.

Change equalization, volume, and other playback settings here (see page 40).

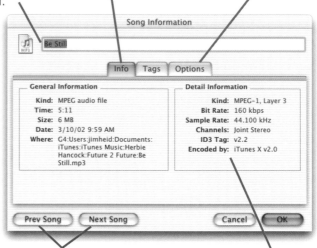

Need to edit information for multiple songs? Rather than repeatedly choosing Get Info, just click Prev Song to display information for the previous song (the one located above the current song in iTunes' window) or Next Song to get info for the next song.

Get the lowdown on a song's encoding format here.

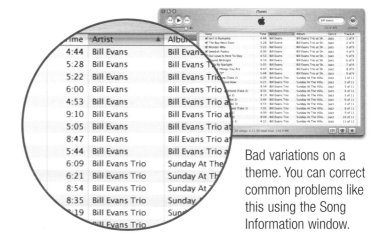

Bad variations on a theme. You can correct common problems like this using the Song Information window.

## How MP3 Files Store Song Information

MP3 files can store more than music. They can also hold *ID3 tags*, which can hold artist, song, and album names as well as release dates, track numbers, genres, and even comments and lyrics. iTunes doesn't provide access to every tidbit that an ID3 tag can hold, but it does let you view and edit the most important ones, as shown here.

# A Power Tool for ID3 Tag Editing

If you do a lot of tag editing or are just curious to see what other kinds of information an ID3 tag can hold, get a copy of Jörg Pressel's ID3X. This Mac OS X program lets you apply tag changes to an entire series of files in one fell swoop. It also supports tags that iTunes doesn't, including those that store lyrics and even scanned images of a CD's cover. You can find ID3X at shareware download sites, such as VersionTracker (www.versiontracker.com).

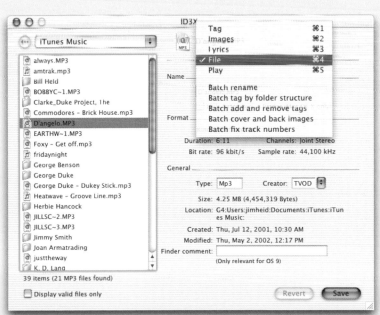

# Sequencing Songs with Playlists

Once you've created a library of MP3s, you'll want to create playlists: collections of songs sequenced in whatever order you like.

You might create playlists whose songs set a mood: Workout Tunes, Road Trip Songs, Romantic Getaway Music.

You might create playlists that play all your favorite tunes from specific artists: The Best of U2, John Coltrane Favorites, The Artistry of Brittany Spears. (That last one is pretty small.)

With playlists, you can mix and match songs in any way you see fit. You can add a song to as many playlists as you like, or even create a playlist that plays one song five times in a row.

Once you've created playlists, you can, of course, play them. But you can also transfer them to an iPod portable player (see page 44) and burn them to create your own compilation CDs (see page 32).

## Step 1:
## Create a New Playlist

To create a new playlist, click the plus sign or choose New Playlist from the File menu.

## Step 2:
## Rename the New Playlist

Type a name for the new playlist.

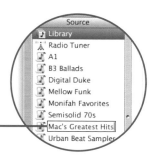

## Step 3:
## Drag Songs to the Playlist

You can drag songs into the playlist one at a time or select a series of songs and drag them all at once. To select a range of songs that are adjacent to each other, use the Shift key: click on the first song, then Shift-click on the last one. To select songs that aren't adjacent to one another, press ⌘ while clicking on each song.

## Viewing and Fine-Tuning a Playlist

To view a playlist's contents, simply click on its name. To change the playlists's name, click again and then edit the name. To delete a playlist, select it and press Delete. (Deleting a playlist *doesn't* delete its songs from your Library.)

To change the playback order of the songs in the playlist, drag songs up or down. Here, the last song in the playlist is being moved to between songs 2 and 3.

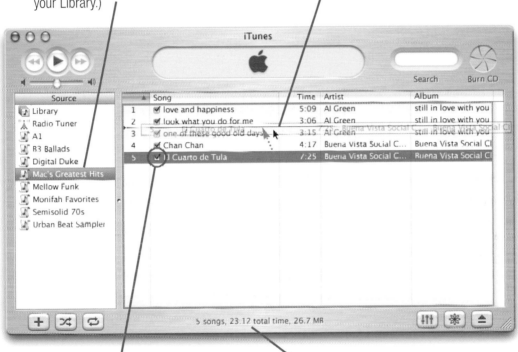

To omit a song from a playlist, select the song and press the Delete key. To omit the song without deleting it— for example, if you want to keep it in the playlist but not burn it or play it back this time—uncheck the box next to the song's name.

iTunes displays the playlist's statistics, including its duration, here.

**Important:** If you're burning an audio CD, keep the playlist's duration under 74 minutes.

# Playlist Tips

## Opening a Playlist in a Separate Window

To open a playlist in its own window, double-click the playlist's name. iTunes opens the playlist in a new window, and switches its main window to the Library view.

You can open as many playlist windows as you like, and drag songs between them, as shown here. It's a handy way to work, since it lets you see the contents of your Library and your playlist at the same time.

## Creating a Playlist From a Selection

Here's a shortcut for creating a playlist: in the Library view, select the songs you want to include in a playlist, and then choose New Playlist From Selection from the File menu. iTunes will add the songs to a new playlist, which you can then rename.

## Naming Playlists with iPod in Mind

If you plan to transfer your playlists to an iPod, there's a trick you can use to ensure that a given playlist will appear at the top of the iPod's Playlist menu. This cuts down on the time and scrolling required to find a given playlist.

To have a playlist appear at the top of the iPod's Playlist menu, precede the playlist's name with a hyphen (-) character, as in - *Mac's Greatest Hits.*

A few other punctuation characters, including period (.), will also send a playlist to the top of the heap.

## Exporting Playlists

In iTunes' Advanced menu, there lurks a command called Export Song List. Select a playlist and choose this command, and iTunes will create a text file containing all the information about each song, from its name to its bit rate. You can open this text file using a word processor, or you can import it into a spreadsheet or database program.

The items—artist, song name, album name, and so on—in an exported playlist are separated by tab characters. (In geek speak, this command creates a tab-delimited text file.) Most spreadsheet and database programs can read these tabs and use them to put each piece of information in its own spreadsheet cell or database field.

# Better Ways to Export Playlists

Too much information! That's what you're likely to say when you open a file created with iTunes' Export Song List command. Maybe you've exported the playlist because you want to create a custom CD label or jewel case card. In such a case, you don't need the bit rate and format of every song, not to mention all the other stuff iTunes includes in the exported file.

Some programmers have created free AppleScripts that provide improved playlist-exporting features. (To learn about expanding iTunes with AppleScripts, see page 42.) The Doug's AppleScripts for iTunes Web site (www.malcolmadams.com/itunes/) contains a great selection, including an AppleScript that will create a Web page showing a playlist's contents.

Choose the information you want to export (right), and the AppleScript creates the Web page (far right).

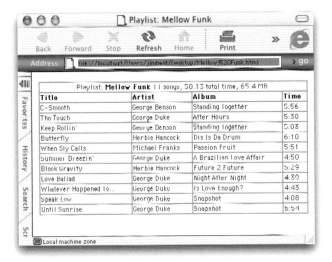

## Other Playlist-Related Scripts

While downloading iTunes AppleScripts from the above Web site, you might want to explore some of the other playlist-related scripts that are available.

One called TuneSpy will create a playlist containing songs you've recently played. It can also create a Daily History playlist containing the songs you play on a given day. It's the Web browser history concept extended to iTunes.

Other scripts will create playlists containing a random assortment of songs, help you import and export

playlists, and much more. Poke around a bit—you'll be surprised at just how powerful iTunes can become when it's supercharged with a few AppleScripts.

# Find that Tune: Searching and Browsing

As your music library grows, you'll want to take advantage of the features iTunes provides for locating songs, artists, and albums.

With the iTunes Search box, you can quickly narrow down the list of songs displayed to only those songs that match the criterion you typed.

With the Browse button, you can quickly scan your music library by artist, album name, or genre.

And with the Show Song File command in the File menu, you can quickly display the actual MP3 file that corresponds to a given song in your library or in a playlist.

## Searching

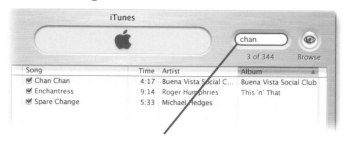

As you type in the Search box, iTunes narrows down the list of songs displayed. iTunes searches the album title, artist, genre, and song title items. To see all the songs in your library or playlist, select the text in the Search box and press Delete.

## Browsing

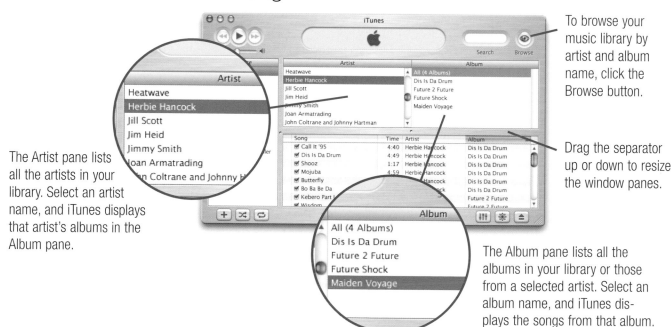

To browse your music library by artist and album name, click the Browse button.

Drag the separator up or down to resize the window panes.

The Artist pane lists all the artists in your library. Select an artist name, and iTunes displays that artist's albums in the Album pane.

The Album pane lists all the albums in your library or those from a selected artist. Select an album name, and iTunes displays the songs from that album.

See iTunes' searching ⦿ 7
and browsing ⦿ 9
features in action.

## Browsing by Genre

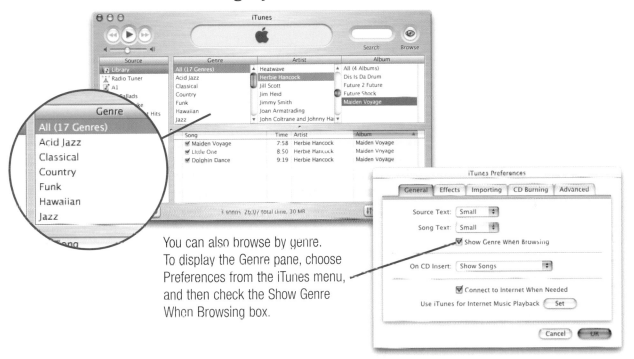

You can also browse by genre.
To display the Genre pane, choose
Preferences from the iTunes menu,
and then check the Show Genre
When Browsing box.

## Finding a Song's MP3 File

There may be times when you want to locate
a song's MP3 file on your hard drive—to back
it up, for example, to move it to another drive,
or to simply determine where it's stored.

To locate a song's disk file, select the song
and choose Show Song File from the File
menu (or press ⌘-R). iTunes switches you to
the Finder, opens the folder containing the
song, and highlights the song file.

# Improving Sound Quality with the Equalizer

The iTunes *equalizer* lets you boost and attenuate various frequency ranges; think of it as a very sophisticated set of bass and treble controls. You might pump up the bass to make up for small speakers. You might boost the high frequencies to make up for aging ears. Or you might increase the mid-range frequencies to improve the clarity of a spoken recording.

The iTunes equalizer (EQ) divides the audio spectrum into ten *bands*, and provides a slider that lets you boost or attenuate frequencies in each band. The bands start at 32 hertz (Hz), a deeper bass than most of us can hear, and go all the way up to 16 kilohertz (kHz), which, while short of dog-whistle territory, approaches the upper limits of human hearing. (If you've been around for more than several decades or have listened to a lot of loud music, 16 kHz is probably out of your hearing range.)

iTunes provides more than 20 equalization presets from which to choose. You can listen to all your music with one setting applied, or you can assign separate settings to individual songs. You can also adjust EQ settings by hand and create your own presets.

To display the equalizer, click the Equalizer button (▥) near the lower-right corner of the iTunes window, or choose Equalizer from the Window menu (⌘-2).

## Finding Your Way Around the Equalizer

Click to turn on the equalizer.

Drag a slider up to boost the frequencies in that range; drag it down to attenuate them.

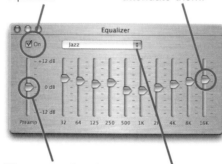

The preamp boosts or attenuates the volume for all frequencies equally.

Choose a preset, create a new preset, or manage your list of presets.

## Creating Your Own Preset

**1.** To save a customized preset, choose Make Preset from the preset pop-up menu.

**2.** Type a name for the preset and click OK.

New Preset Name:

Death Bass

The new preset appears in the pop-up menu.

See the iTunes equalizer in action, and see how to apply EQ settings to individual songs  11.

## Assigning Presets to Individual Songs

If you've turned on the equalizer, iTunes applies the current EQ setting to any song you play back. However, you can also assign EQ settings on a song-by-song basis.

First, choose View Options from the Edit menu, and then check the Equalizer box.

Next, choose the desired preset from the pop-up menu in the Equalizer column.

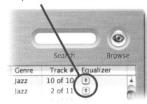

To change the EQ settings for several songs at once, select the songs and choose Get Info from the File menu. Then choose the desired EQ setting.

## Presets that Make You Smile

You may have noticed that many of iTunes' presets have a smile-like appearance: the low- and high-frequency ranges are boosted to a greater degree than the mid-range frequencies.

Classical

Audio gurus call this shape the Fletcher-Munson curve. It reflects the fact that, at most listening levels, our ears are less sensitive to low and high frequencies than they are to mid-range frequencies.

Jazz

Chances are your stereo system has a Loudness button. When you turn it on, the stereo applies a similar curve to make the music sound more natural at lower volume levels.

Rock

Latin

## "That Song Needs a Bit More 250"

Being able to control the volume of 10 different frequency ranges is great, but how do you know which ranges to adjust? Here's a guide to how frequency ranges correlate with those of some common musical instruments and the human voice. Note that these ranges don't take into account harmonics, which are the tonal complexities that help us discern between instruments. Harmonics can easily exceed 20 kHz.

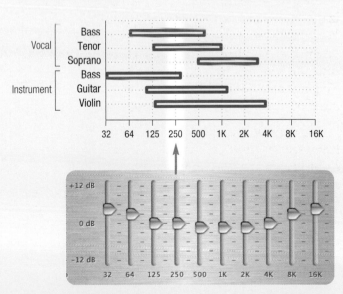

# Burning CDs

After you've created some playlists, you can burn their songs onto audio CDs that will play in just about any CD player. (Some older CD and DVD players have trouble reading discs created using a CD burner.)

Burning a CD using iTunes is a two-click proposition. But there are some subtleties behind CD burning that you may want to explore.

## Step 1:
## Select the Playlist You Want to Burn

If the playlist contains a song that you don't want to burn, uncheck the box next to the song's name.

iTunes displays the playlist's total duration here.

**Important:** If you're burning an audio CD, keep the playlist's duration under 74 minutes.

## Step 2:
## Click the Burn CD button

When you click Burn CD, iTunes opens your Mac's CD tray and instructs you to insert a blank CD.

To cancel the burn, click here.

## Step 3:
## Begin the Burn

iTunes displays the number of songs it will burn and their total duration.

To begin burning, click Burn CD again.

As the CD burns, iTunes displays a status message. You can cancel a burn in progress by clicking the ⊗ button, but you'll end up with a *coaster*—a damaged CD blank whose only useful purpose is to sit beneath a cold drink.

Watch the CD-burning process, and see how to print and apply labels for CDs ⊙ 12-13.

# Tips for Your Burning Endeavors

## CD-R Details

Many brands of CD-R media are available, and some people swear by a given brand. Some users even claim that certain colors of CD-R blank are better than others.

My advice: Don't sweat it—just buy name-brand CD-R blanks. And don't fret about their colors. Color varies depending on the organic dyes used by the CD-R's manufacturer, and different manufacturers use different dye formulations. Color isn't a useful indicator of CD-R quality anyway.

Some CD-R manufacturers offer "high-capacity" media capable of storing 80 minutes of audio, or about 703MB. Ninety-minute media are also available. Think twice about using these high-capacity media. To achieve the higher capacity, high-capacity media pack tracks closer together, and some CD players may not be able to read them successfully.

How long will your burned CDs last? Manufacturers toss out figures ranging from 75 to 200 years, but these are only estimates based on accelerated aging tests that attempt to simulate the effects of time.

One thing is certain: a CD-R will last longer when kept away from heat and bright light. Avoid scratching *either side* of a CD-R—use a felt-tipped pen to label it, and don't write any more than you need to. (The solvents in the ink can damage the CD over time.)

To learn more about CD-R media, visit the CD-Recordable FAQ at www.cdrfaq.org.

## Burning MP3 CDs

Normally, iTunes burns CDs in standard audio CD format. But you can also burn tracks as MP3 files; this lets you take advantage of MP3's compression so you can squeeze more music onto a CD—roughly ten times the number of songs that an audio CD will hold.

But there's a catch: Most audio CD players can't play MP3-format CDs. If you're shopping for a CD or DVD player, you may want to look for one that supports MP3 playback.

To have iTunes burn in MP3 format, first choose Preferences from the iTunes menu, and choose the CD Burning tab. Click the MP3 CD button, and then click OK.

## Setting the Gap Between Tracks

Normally, iTunes uses two-second gaps to separate songs on an audio CD. But there may be times when you want to change that gap or remove it entirely—for example, many contemporary artists sequence the songs on their CDs so that one seamlessly flows into the next; a two-second gap would ruin that mood.

To change the gap, choose the desired setting from the Gap Between Songs pop-up menu in the CD Burning tab of the iTunes Preferences dialog box.

## Burning to CD-RW Media

For broadest compatibility with CD players, you'll want to burn using CD-R blanks, which can't be erased and reused. But the CD burners in all current Macs can also use CD-RW media—*rewritable* media—which costs more but can be erased and reused again and again.

A growing number of CD players can play back rewritable media, and if yours is among them, you might consider using rewritable media for some burning jobs. Maybe you've recorded some streaming Internet radio for a long car trip, programs you'll only want to hear once. Or perhaps you're creating a one-time playlist for a party. CD-RW is ideal for tasks like these.

Note that iTunes can't erase a CD-RW disc. To do that, use Mac OS X's Disk Utility program; it's located in the Utilities folder, inside the Applications folder.

# Tuning In to Internet Radio

The Internet is transforming a lot of things, and broadcasting is one of them. You can tune into thousands of streaming Internet radio stations using iTunes and other programs.

Many of these stations are commercial or public broadcasters that are also making their audio available on the 'net. But most stations are Internet-only affairs, often set up by music lovers who simply want to share their tastes with the rest of us. You can join them, as described on page 36.

If part of streaming audio's appeal is its diversity, the other part is its immediacy. Streaming playback begins just a few seconds after you click on a link—there's no waiting for huge sound files to download before you hear a single note.

Several formats for streaming audio exist, and MP3 is one of them. Using the iTunes Radio Tuner, you can listen to Internet radio stations that stream in MP3 format.

You can't use iTunes to listen to Internet radio stations that use formats other than MP3. To tune in the full range of Internet streaming media, use Apple's QuickTime Player (www.apple.com/quicktime), Microsoft's Windows Media Player (www.windowsmedia.com), and RealNetworks' RealPlayer (www.real.com).

## Turn on the Tuner

The first step in using iTunes to listen to Internet radio is to activate the iTunes Radio Tuner.

Click Radio Tuner to switch the iTunes view to the radio tuner. To display the tuner in its own window, double-click.

iTunes retrieves its list of Internet radio categories and stations from the Internet. Click Refresh to have iTunes contact the tuning service and update its list of categories and stations.

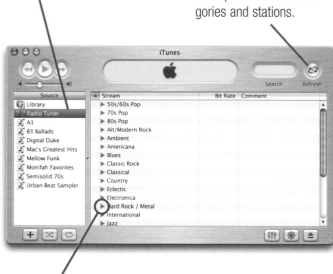

iTunes groups Internet radio stations by genre; to display the stations in a genre, double-click the genre name or click on the triangle to its left.

## Bandwidth:
## Internet Radio's Antenna

The quality of your Internet radio "reception" depends in part on the speed of your Internet connection.

With Internet radio, information listed in the Bit Rate column is particularly important. It reflects not only how much the audio has been compressed, but also how fast a connection you'll need in order to listen without interruption. For example, if you have a 56 kbps modem connection, you won't be able to listen to a stream whose bit rate is higher than 56 kbps. (Indeed, even a 56 kbps stream may hiccup occasionally.)

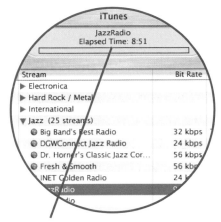

iTunes shows how long you've been listening to a stream. Notice that when you're listening to a live stream, there is no control for skipping forward and backward within a song.

To listen to a station, double-click the station's name.

## How Streaming Works

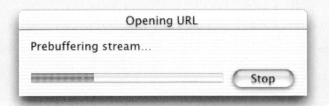

When you begin playing back an Internet radio stream, iTunes connects to a streaming server, which downloads several seconds' worth of audio into an area of memory called a buffer. When the buffer is full, playback begins. The player then contin-

ues downloading audio into the buffer while simultaneously playing back the audio that it has already buffered. It's this just-in-time downloading that gives streaming its near-immediate gratification—most of the time, anyway.

If Internet congestion or connection problems interrupt the incoming stream, the buffer

may empty completely, stalling playback while the buffer refills.

# Internet Radio: The Rest of the Story

Do you want to go from being a listener to being a broadcaster? The easiest way to set up your own Internet radio station is to use the Live365 broadcasting service (www.live365.com).

For a monthly fee of under $10, Live365 will dish out up to 100MB worth of MP3 tracks. You upload your tracks to Live365's servers, create playlists, and just like that, you're a broadcaster. Your station might even end up in the iTunes Radio Tuner listing.

If you have a fast, continuous Internet connection, you can also run your own streaming server and dish out MP3s directly from your iTunes music library. Apple's free QuickTime Streaming Server can serve up MP3 files, and any Internet user with an MP3 program—iTunes, RealPlayer, WinAmp, and so on—will be able to tune in.

You can download the QuickTime Streaming Server at www.apple.com/quicktime/products/qtss/. But take note: while the server is well designed, setting it up isn't as straightforward as using iTunes or the other digital hub programs.

You configure and monitor the free QuickTime Streaming Server using your Web browser. Note that operating your own streaming server may require you to pay licensing fees to the copyright holders of the music you broadcast. For details on the licensing controversies swirling around Internet radio, see www.saveinternetradio.org.

You can also use QuickTime Streaming Server to set up a "local" radio station that broadcasts on your home or office network. Using the QuickTime Streaming Server administrator screens, configure your media directory to be your iTunes Music folder. Then you can create QuickTime Streaming Server playlists and tune in your music from any computer on your network.

## Internet Radio and Playlists

You can drag Internet radio station listings into playlists as though they were standalone MP3 tracks. Because Internet radio stations broadcast continuously, iTunes won't switch from one station to the next when it plays back the playlist.

Still, an Internet radio playlist can be a handy way to create a list of favorite Internet radio stations. Drag your favorite stations into a playlist, and you can access them with one mouse click—no need to activate the Radio Tuner and then open various genres to find the station you want.

## Recording Internet Radio Streams

Internet radio streams aren't saved on your hard drive—like conventional radio, Internet radio is a fleeting phenomenon.

Or is it? The truth is, there are a couple of ways you can record Internet radio streams. The easiest way is to use Johann Huguenin's iNet Stream Archiver. With this $15 shareware program, you can create bookmarks of your favorite Internet radio stations by dragging the stations' listings from the iTunes window. You can then record their streams on your hard drive, optionally using a timer function to start and stop recording.

iNet Stream Archiver is limited to recording MP3 streams. To record streams in other formats—for example, QuickTime or Microsoft Windows Media—you can use an audio-recording utility such as N2MP3 Professional, described on page 39. Using a cable with a ⅛-inch stereo miniplug at each end, connect your Mac's speaker jack to its audio-input jack (or to the audio-input jack on a USB audio adapter such as Griffin Technology's iMic).

Start iTunes (or any other streaming player), and adjust its playback volume so that your

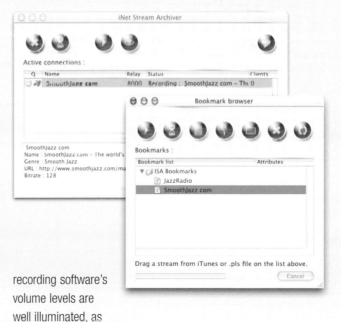

recording software's volume levels are well illuminated, as described on the following pages. Finally, begin recording.

# Analog to Digital: Converting Tapes and Albums

If you're like me, you're desperate to recapture the past: you want to create MP3 files from audio cassettes and vinyl albums.

Bridging the gap between the analog and digital worlds requires some software and hardware. The process involves connecting your Mac to an audio source, such as a cassette deck or stereo system, and then using recording software to save the audio on your hard drive as it plays back. You can encode the resulting files into MP3 format and add them to your iTunes music library.

Depending on your Mac, you may need an audio-input adapter in order to connect an audio source to the computer. Of current Mac models, only two—Apple's 2002 PowerBook G4 and the eMac—contain audio-input jacks. If you have a different model, you'll need an adapter such as Griffin Technology's iMic (above), which is inexpensive and does a fine job.

## Step 1: Make the Connections

Recording analog sources is easiest when you connect the Mac to the audio output of a stereo system. This will enable you to record anything your stereo can play, from vinyl albums to cassettes to FM radio.

Most stereo receivers have auxiliary output jacks on their back panels. To make the connection, use a cable with two RCA phono plugs on one end and a ⅛-inch stereo miniplug on the other. Connect the phono plugs to the receiver's output jacks, and the miniplug to the input jack on your Mac or audio adapter.

## Step 2: Prepare to Record

Before you record, set your audio levels properly: you want the audio signal to be as loud as possible without distorting the sound.

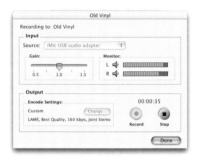

Fire up your audio recording software (N2MP3 Professional is shown here), and adjust its recording levels so that the loudest passages of music fully illuminate the volume meters.

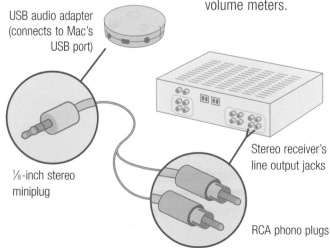

USB audio adapter (connects to Mac's USB port)

⅛-inch stereo miniplug

Stereo receiver's line output jacks

RCA phono plugs

## Step 3: Record

First, do a test recording. Activate your software's Record mode and begin playing back the original audio, preferably a loud passage. After a minute or two, stop and play back the recorded audio to verify that the recording levels you set are correct. Listen for distortion in loud passages; if you hear any, decrease the levels slightly.

Once you've arrived at the correct setting for recording levels, record the original audio in its entirety.

## Step 4: Encode as MP3

If you aren't recording directly to MP3 format, you'll need to convert the recording (which is likely in AIFF format) into MP3 format. You can use iTunes to do this: choose Convert to MP3 from the Advanced menu, and then locate and double-click on the recording you just made. iTunes will convert the track and store the resulting MP3 file in your iTunes library.

iTunes can also convert multiple tracks in one operation. After choosing Convert to MP3, simply ⌘-click on each file you want to import.

Before converting, you might want to adjust iTunes' encoding settings by using the Preferences command as described on page 18. Some MP3 buffs lower the bit rate for music that originated on analog media, on the theory that a higher bit rate would be wasted on it. You might try a bit rate of 96 kbps, with VBR turned on. Consider doing some tests and letting your ears be the judge.

## Choosing an Audio Recording Program

Plenty of audio-recording programs are available, ranging from free programs such as TC Works' SparkME to commercial programs such as Bias' Peak.

A fine utility for recording analog audio is Proteron Software's N2MP3 Professional. This powerhouse program can record directly into MP3 format, thus saving you an additional step. It also includes several MP3 encoders, including one called

LAME, whose sound quality many MP3 gurus prefer to the encoder built into iTunes. You can also use N2MP3 Professional to record Internet streaming radio, as described on page 37.

One of my favorite programs for recording analog audio is CD Spin Doctor, included with Roxio's Toast Titanium CD burning software. CD Spin Doctor creates AIFF files, which you

can encode into MP3 format using iTunes.

A few features make CD Spin Doctor particularly ideal for converting analog recordings into digital form. One is the Auto-Define Tracks command: choose it, and CD Spin Doctor scans a recording, detects the silence between each song, and then divides the recording into multiple tracks. This makes it easy to record one side of an

album and then divvy it up into separate tracks.

CD Spin Doctor has noise and pop filters that can clean up abused records, as well as an "exciter" filter that enhances old recordings by beefing up bass and improving the sense of stereo separation.

You'll find links to these and other audio programs on *The Macintosh Digital Hub* Web site.

# iTunes Tips

## Crossfading Between Songs

You hear it on the radio all the time: as one song nears its end, it begins to fade as the next song starts to play. You can recreate this effect in iTunes. First, choose Preferences from the iTunes menu, click the Effects tab, and then check the Crossfade Playback box.

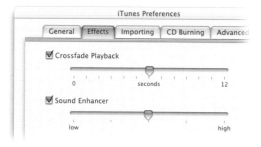

Use the slider to adjust the length of the crossfade effect.

With crossfading, one song fades out...

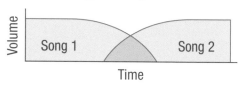

...as the next song fades in.

## Using the Sound Enhancer

You can add aural punch by improving what audio gurus call *presence*, the perception that the instruments are right in the room with you. To do this, use the Sound Enhancer option in the Effects tab of the Preferences dialog box. Drag the slider toward the High setting, and you may notice brighter-sounding high frequencies and an enhanced sense of stereo separation. Experiment with the setting that sounds best for your ears—and your audio equipment.

## Adjusting a Song's Volume Level

When you create a playlist containing songs from numerous albums, you may notice some songs are louder than others. You can compensate for this by adjusting the playback volume for specific songs. First, Control-click on a song and then choose Get Info from the contextual pop-up menu.

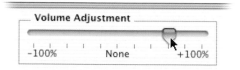

In the Options tab of the Song Information dialog box, drag the Volume Adjustment slider to decrease or increase the song's playback volume.

# Tips for the iTunes Library

## Adding MP3s from Other Sources

Chances are most of the MP3s you work with will be ones you've created from your own audio CDs. But you can also buy downloadable MP3 tracks from music sites such as MP3.com; many music sites also offer free MP3s.

And, although record industry executives wouldn't want me to say so, you can also download MP3s using utilities such as LimeWire (www.limewire.com) to access file-sharing networks such as Gnutella. Note that downloading via Gnutella may make you a thief—most of the tracks available through file-swapping networks have been shared without the permission of their copyright holders.

Regardless of where your other MP3s come from, you can add them to your iTunes music library by simply dragging them

into the iTunes window or by using the File menu's Add to Library command. To avoid having MP3s scattered all over your hard drive, you might want to move these files to your iTunes Music folder before dragging them into the iTunes window.

## Accessing Your Music from a Different Mac

If you have multiple Macs on a network, you can make one Mac's iTunes music library accessible to other Macs on your network. On the Mac containing your music library, make an alias of the iTunes Music Library (2) file, and then turn on file sharing using the Sharing item in System Preferences. (For more details, search the Mac's online help for *file sharing*.)

On the other Macs, delete or rename the iTunes Music Library (2) file. (If you've already assembled a music library on those Macs, rename their

copies of the iTunes Music Library (2) file or move the file to a different folder.) Next, copy the alias you created to the other Macs, storing it in the iTunes folder within the Documents folder. Finally, rename the alias as iTunes Music Library (2).

To access the music library on the server Mac (the one with file sharing on), first connect to the server and then start up iTunes. Because the alias on each Mac is pointing to the original iTunes music library, each Mac will be able to access the songs on the server Mac.

This library-sharing technique is one of those undocumented, use-at-your-own-risk tips. It does work most of the time, although I've noticed that iTunes sometimes acts flaky when it's accessing a music library stored elsewhere. Be sure to connect to the server Mac before starting up iTunes on any of the client Macs.

## Library Management Scripts

Several useful AppleScripts are available for automating and enhancing iTunes. You'll also find some great scripts aimed at managing the iTunes music library. For example, a script called iTunes Library Manager makes it easy to back up the iTunes Music Library (2) file so you can, for example, save multiple copies of various playlists. For details on downloading and installing AppleScripts for iTunes, see page 42.

# Adding On: Scripts and Beyond

I've already mentioned that you can enhance the capabilities of iTunes through AppleScripts that automate iTunes in various ways.

You can also enhance the iTunes visualizer—the feature that displays those psychedelic patterns as your music plays back—by adding plug-ins. Visualizer plug-ins may not be as practical as AppleScripts, but on-screen psychedelics can often be more fun than practicalities.

Here's how to download and install iTunes AppleScripts and visualizer plug-ins, as well as information on some other programs that can round out the audio spoke of your digital hub.

## Visualize Cool Graphics

If you're a fan of the iTunes visualizer, try out some of the free visualizer plug-ins available on the Web. My favorite is Andy O'Meara's free G-Force, which goes well beyond the built-in iTunes visualizer. For example, you can "play" G-Force—controlling its patterns and colors—by pressing keys on your keyboard as a song plays back.

You can find G-Force and other visualizer plug-ins by going to download Web sites.

Most visualizers include installation programs that tuck the plug-ins into the appropriate spot. But, just for the record, iTunes visualizer plug-ins generally live within the iTunes folder of your Library folder.

## Automating with AppleScript

AppleScript is a powerful automation technology that is part of the Mac OS and many Mac programs, including iTunes. AppleScript puts your Mac on autopilot: when you run a script, its commands can control one or more programs and make them perform a series of steps.

Dozens of useful scripts are available for iTunes. You might start by downloading the set of scripts created by Apple (www.apple.com/applescript/itunes). After you've experimented with them, sprint to Doug's AppleScripts for iTunes (www.malcolmadams.com/itunes), where you'll find the best collection of iTunes AppleScripts.

After you've downloaded an iTunes AppleScript, you need to move it to a specific place in order for iTunes to recognize it. First, quit iTunes. Then, click the Home button or choose Home from the Finder's Go menu. Next, locate and open the Library folder, and then locate and open the iTunes folder. Create a folder named Scripts inside this folder and stash your scripts here.

See iTunes AppleScripts ◎ **14**,
the G-Force visualizer ◎ **15**,
and some hardware add-ons ◎ **16-21**.

# Beyond iTunes: Completing Your Audio Arsenal

Several programs can work with iTunes to expand its capabilities. I've mentioned some in previous sections—N2MP3 Professional, iNet Stream Archiver, and LimeWire, for example. A few more favorites are described here; for links to even more audio add-ons, visit *The Macintosh Digital Hub* Web site.

## iHam on iRye

Obviously named by over-caffeinated programmers, iHam on iRye is an interesting program that lets you control iTunes from a different Mac—think of it as a remote control for iTunes. First, set up the iHam on iRye server on the Mac containing iTunes and your music library. You can then use the iHam on iRye client program to connect to the server and play back songs and playlists. iPickles sold separately.

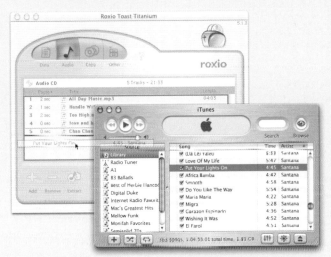

## Toast Titanium

Roxio's Toast Titanium is a burning program for serious CD arsonists. This application can burn DVDs as well as audio and data CDs, and provides more control over the burning process. Just one example: while iTunes puts the same amount of time between each song on a CD, Toast Titanium lets you specify a

different interval for each song. Toast Titanium also includes the CD Spin Doctor audio-recording program discussed on page 39.

Toast also works together with iTunes. As shown above, you can drag and drop songs from iTunes directly into Toast.

## Panic's Audion

Audion combines ripping, play-back, Internet radio, powerful playlist features, visualizers, and CD burning into one program. Sound like iTunes? Audion goes well beyond. For example, Audion supports a variety of MP3 encoders, rather than just one. It also lets you slow down the playback of a song—handy for musicians trying to figure out a complicated riff. Audion lets you play back two MP3s simultaneously and mix between them. With Audion's Alarm Clock command, you can have a song or playlist wake you up.

There's much more to Audion than I've described here. Suffice it to say that if you're into MP3, you should download the free trial version and audition Audion.

Beethoven R...,968 bytes
851,968 bytes

# iPod: Music to Go

It's hard to appreciate the significance of the iPod until you load it up with hundreds of songs and begin carrying it around with you.

Then it hits you: all of your favorite songs are right there with you, ready to play—in the car, on a walk, in the living room, on a plane. There's no finding and fumbling with CDs, and every song is only a couple of button presses away.

Several factors work together to make the iPod the best portable music player, starting with its capacity: no other portable player of its size can store as many tunes.

Another factor is the iPod's integration with iTunes: connect the iPod to your Mac, and iTunes automatically synchronizes your music library and playlists. And, the synchronization occurs over FireWire, which is many times faster than the USB connections used by other portable players.

And finally, there's the iPod's versatility. Its ability to store contact information and other files make the iPod more than a portable music player.

## Life with an iPod

### Step 1: Build a Music Library

Use the techniques described earlier in this section to import songs from audio CDs, assign equalization settings (optional), edit song information (if necessary), and create playlists.

### Step 2: Transfer to the iPod

Connect the iPod to your Mac using the included FireWire cable. iTunes copies your music library and playlists to the iPod.

While the iPod is connected, its battery charges. The battery charges to 80 percent of its capacity in an hour, and charges fully in about three hours.

You can adjust settings for updating the music on your iPod by using the iPod Preferences dialog box, described on the following pages.

Watch an iPod synchronization session ⦿ **17** and see an iPod carrying case and other accessories ⦿ **19-21**.

## Step 3: Listen and Repeat

Disconnect the iPod and start listening. When you modify your iTunes music library or playlists, you can update the iPod's contents to match by simply connecting the iPod again.

You can use the headphones jack to connect the iPod to a stereo system or other audio hardware, such as the FM transmitter shown on the DVD. To connect to a stereo system, use a cable with a ⅛-inch miniplug on one end and two RCA phono plugs on the other. Connect the phono plugs to an available input on the back of your system.

To the right of the iPod's audio-output jack is the Hold button. Slide it to the left to disable the iPod's buttons. This is useful when you're transporting the iPod in a briefcase or purse, where its buttons could get pressed, causing the battery to drain.

The battery gauge shows how much power remains.

The iPod's menu system uses a "drill-down" scheme: select an option and press the Select button, and you drill down one level to another menu or list of choices.

To back up to the previous list of choices, press the Menu button.

Use the scroll wheel to move the menu highlight up and down, and to adjust the playback volume.

To skip to the previous or next song, press the Previous or Next button.

To pause and resume playback, press the Play/Pause button. To turn off the iPod, press and hold this button for a few seconds.

To choose an item in a menu, press the Select button.

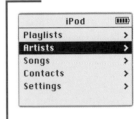

# Setting iPod Preferences

Normally, iTunes will synchronize all your playlists and your entire music library, or at least as much of it as will fit on the iPod.

But there may be times when you want to manually control which playlists and songs iTunes copies to the iPod. Maybe your iTunes music library is larger than will fit on the iPod, requiring you to specify what you want to copy. Or maybe you listen to some songs on your Mac but not on your iPod, and you don't want to waste iPod disk space by copying those songs.

Whatever the reason, you can use the iPod Preferences dialog box to specify updating preferences.

You can also use this dialog box to activate *FireWire disk mode*, in which the iPod appears on your desktop just like a hard drive (which, of course, it is). In FireWire disk mode, you can use the Mac's Finder to copy files to and from the iPod's hard drive. This is a handy way to shuttle documents to and from work, or to carry backups of important programs or files with you on the road.

**iPoodle**

## Opening iPod Preferences

When you connect the iPod to the Mac and start iTunes, the iPod appears in the Source pane of the iTunes window, and an iPod preferences icon appears next to the Equalizer button.

The graph shows how much iPod disk space you've used and how much remains.

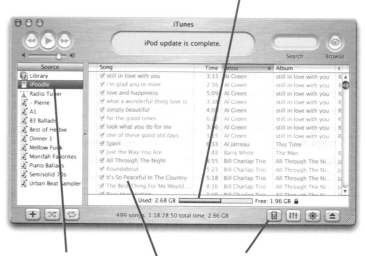

To rename the iPod, click its name and then type a new name. The name appears in iTunes, as shown above, and in the Finder (left) when the iPod is in FireWire disk mode. It also appears in the iPod's Info screen.

To display the iPod Preferences dialog box, click the Options button (🔘).

If iTunes is configured to update automatically (below), the iPod's contents appear dimmed (above) and you can't manually change them.

**iPod Preferences**

◉ Automatically update all songs and playlists
○ Automatically update selected playlists only:

## iPod Preferences Settings

To control which playlists are copied, click this option and check the box next to each playlist you want to copy.

Normally, iTunes copies everything when you connect the iPod.

To update songs and playlists by hand, click this option. After you click OK, the iPod's contents in the iTunes window are no longer dimmed, and you can drag songs and playlists from iTunes to the iPod. See "Manual Management" on page 48.

To have your Mac automatically start iTunes when you connect the iPod, choose this option.

To use the iPod as a FireWire hard drive, choose this option. (You must do so to add contacts and notes to the iPod; see page 50.)

**iPod Preferences**

- ● Automatically update all songs and playlists
- ○ Automatically update selected playlists only:
  - ☐ – Pierre
  - ☐ A1
  - ☐ B3 Ballads
  - ☐ Best of Herbie
  - ☐ Dinner 1
- ○ Manually manage songs and playlists

- ☑ Open iTunes when attached
- ☑ Enable FireWire disk use
- ☐ Only update checked songs

Cancel    OK

If you've chosen automatic updating but don't want to copy all new songs to the iPod, check this box and then, in the Library, uncheck any new songs that you do not want copied. When you next update the iPod, only the new songs that are checked will be copied to it.

# iPod Tips

Here are some tips for getting more out of your iPod and appreciating its finer points.

## Browsing by Album

Looking for a way to access songs by album? It isn't obvious, but it's there: go to Artists, then select All.

## Scrubbing within a Song

You can quickly move around, or scrub, within a song while it plays. Press the Select button, and the elapsed-time gauge on the iPod's screen is replaced with a little diamond—just like the one iTunes displays during playback. Using the scroll wheel, move the diamond left and right to scrub within the song.

## Extending Battery Life

To get the longest playing times, turn off the screen's backlighting, avoid jumping between songs frequently (the hard drive is one of the iPod's biggest power consumers), and use the Settings menu to turn off the iPod's equalizer. And remember, you can play songs when the iPod is plugged in to its power adapter. If you put the iPod in manual-updating mode or use one of the iPod utilities discussed here, you can even play songs while the iPod is connected to the Mac.

## iPod Utilities

Apple built a simple anti-piracy system into the iPod: its music files are stored in an invisible folder on the iPod's hard drive. Thus, you can't use the Finder to copy music files from the iPod to your hard drive. Music transfer is a one-way street: from the Mac to the iPod.

However, several free or inexpensive utilities let you directly access the MP3 files on an iPod. I'm fond of Flying Mouse Software's PodMaster 1000 ($8). It lets you access the MP3s on an iPod's hard drive, play them back, and view their ID3 tags.

Other direct-access utilities for Mac OS X include Podestal, PodUtil, and iPod2iTunes, all of which are available on software-download sites.

## Manual Management

When you have the iPod set up for manual updating, you can use iTunes to create playlists that exist only on the iPod. In the Source area of the iTunes window, select the iPod and then create the new playlist.

When manual updating is active, you must manually unmount the iPod when you're done with it. You can do this in iTunes (select the iPod in the Source list and then click the Eject button) or by using the Finder (drag the iPod's icon to the Trash or select it and press ⌘-E).

If you ever decide to switch back to iTunes' automatic updating mode, iTunes will replace the iPod's contents with the current music library and playlists.

## Playing While Charging

When the iPod is connected to the Mac, its menus aren't available, preventing you from playing music located on the iPod. One way to work around this is to put the iPod in manual-updating mode, as described previously. You can then play tunes on the iPod by using the iTunes window. The other technique is to use a direct-access utility such as PodMaster 1000, which can play songs directly from the iPod regardless of the current iTunes updating mode.

## iPod Meets Windows

If you have a Windows computer with a FireWire port (which may be called i.Link or 1394), you can connect the iPod and use it as a FireWire hard drive. (If the iPod doesn't appear, it may be because the Windows computer's FireWire port doesn't provide power. Try forcing the iPod into FireWire disk mode by restarting, then immediately holding down Previous and Next.)

With the right software, you can also use a Windows computer to manage an iPod's music library. Windows programs that support music transfer to the iPod include MediaFour Corporation's XPlay (www.mediafour.com) and Joe Master's EphPod (www.ephpod.com).

## FireWire Disk Mode

FireWire disk mode is not only convenient for shuttling documents between two locations, it's also handy for storing often-used programs. For example, you might stash a direct-access utility such as Podestal on your iPod so you can conveniently copy songs to your Mac at home and at the office.

You can even install the Mac OS on an iPod and use the iPod to boot up your Mac. Apple doesn't officially support this, though, and the frequent hard drive access required by the Mac OS could cause the iPod to overheat.

## iPod Key Sequences

| To Do This | Do This |
| --- | --- |
| Turn off the iPod | Hold down Play/Pause for two seconds. |
| Restart the iPod | Hold down Menu and Play/Pause until the Apple logo appears on the screen (five to 10 seconds). |
| Force the iPod into FireWire disk mode (useful if you're using an old Mac or Windows PC containing a non-powered FireWire add-on card) | Restart (see above), then immediately hold down Previous and Next. |
| Have the iPod scan its hard drive for problems | Restart, then immediately hold down Previous, Next, Menu, and Select. Note: Don't jostle the iPod during disk scanning. |
| Have the iPod perform self-diagnostic tests | Restart, then immediately hold down Previous, Next, and Select. |
| Play the built-in Breakout game | Go to Settings > Legal and hold down Select. |

# iPod as Address Book and More

You can store more than just music on your iPod. You can also store names and addresses and short text notes.

The iPod's address book feature is made possible by an Internet standard called vCard. All current email programs support vCard, as do Palm- and PocketPC-based hand-held computers, and even some cell phones.

Mac programmers, intrepid folks that they are, have taken the vCard ball and run with it. Numerous utilities are available that let you peck out notes and store them in vCard format, or that let you convert notes and calendar entries from Microsoft Entourage into vCard format. So your iPod's Contacts menu isn't just an address book—it can store any text tidbits you want.

Before you can add vCards to your iPod, you must activate the iPod's FireWire disk mode. With the iPod connected, open iTunes and click the iPod Preferences button. In the iPod Preferences dialog box, check the Enable FireWire Disk Use box. Remember to remove the iPod's icon from your desktop before disconnecting the iPod from your Mac.

## Adding Contacts from Microsoft Entourage X

In order for the iPod to recognize vCards, you must store them in the iPod's Contacts folder. To copy contacts from Microsoft Entourage to the iPod, open Entourage X's address book and select the contacts you want to copy to the iPod. Next, drag those contacts to the iPod's Contacts folder.

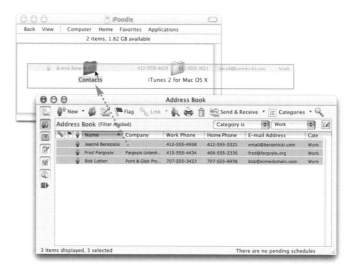

## Deleting Contacts

To remove contacts from the iPod, open the Contacts folder, select the contacts you don't want, and drag them to the Trash.

## Just the Text

Jonathan Chaffer's iPod Text Editor is simplicity itself: type a note title and text, then save the note as a contact.

## iPod Scripts

Apple has created some AppleScripts that convert Microsoft Entourage address books into vCard format, import contacts from the Palm Desktop application into an iPod, and more. Get the scripts at www.apple.com/applescript/ipod.

## All the News That's Fit to Pod

PodNews is an ambitious (and free) utility that downloads news, sports scores, horoscopes, and other information from the Internet, converts it into vCards, and then transfers it to your iPod.

## The iPod's Entourage

Michael Zapp has created programs that export calendar events and email messages from Microsoft Entourage X, enabling you to check your calendar and read email on your iPod.

## Miniature Marvel: Inside the iPod

No other portable music player combines high capacity, small size, and ease of use as effectively as Apple's iPod.

The single most expensive component in the iPod is its Toshiba hard drive, which uses a 1.8-inch disk platter and is available in 5GB or 10GB capacities. Because music is loaded from the hard drive into the iPod's memory, the drive spins only occasionally, making possible the iPod's long battery life.

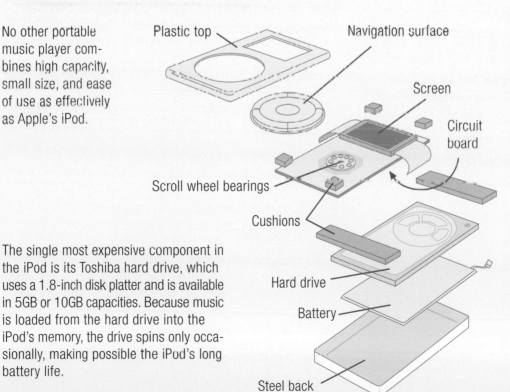

The iPod's LCD screen sits atop a main circuit board that contains 32MB of memory, as well as circuitry that handles playback, FireWire communications, and more.

The iPod's lithium-ion battery is three millimeters thick and manufactured by Sony Corp.

# iPhoto:
# Organizing and
# Sharing Images

## The Macintosh
## Digital Hub

# iPhoto at a Glance

Millions of photographs lead lives of loneliness, trapped in unorganized boxes, where they're never seen. Their digital brethren often share the same fate, exiled to cluttered folders on a hard drive and rarely opened.

With iPhoto, you can free your photos—and organize, print, and share them, too. iPhoto simplifies the entire process. You begin by importing images from a digital camera, your hard drive, or other source. Then you can create albums, organizing the images in whatever order you want.

Along the way, you might also use iPhoto's editing features to improve brightness and contrast, remove red-eye, and crop out unwanted portions of images. And you might use iPhoto's keyword features to help you file and locate images.

When you've finished organizing and editing images, you can share them in several ways, from printing them to publishing them to creating on-screen slide shows.

Welcome to the Photo Liberation Society.

Add an album.  Play a slide show.  View information.  Rotate images.

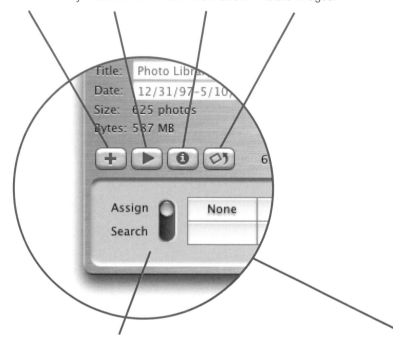

This window pane changes depending on which mode button you've selected. In Organize mode, shown here, you can assign keywords and comments to photos, as well as search for photos (page 70).

See iPhoto and digital photography accessories in action ⊙ 22.

The Photo Library contains all the images you import into iPhoto, whether from a digital camera or a disk file (page 58). Each set of images you import is called a *roll*.

To quickly see the last set of images you imported, click Last Import.

You can assemble photos into albums, and then share the albums (page 64).

You can name each roll of images. To show a roll's images, click on the triangle next to the roll's name. Click the triangle again to hide the images.

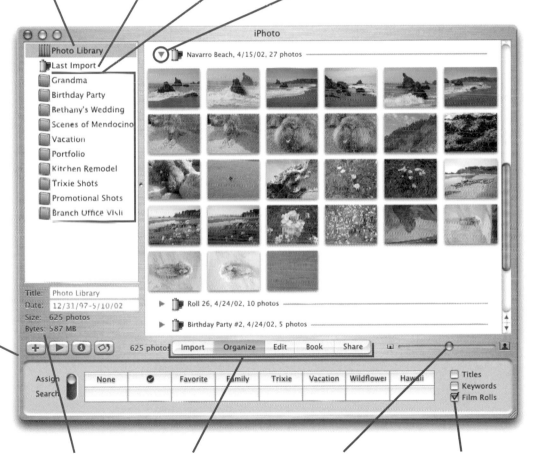

You can view and edit information and comments for images or entire rolls (page 60).

These five buttons switch between each of iPhoto's primary modes.

To change the size of the photos displayed in iPhoto's window, drag the size slider.

Use these check boxes to specify the information you want to see as you browse and organize photos.

# The Essentials of Digital Imaging

Like the digital audio world and other specialized fields, digital imaging has its own jargon and technical concepts to understand. You can accomplish a lot in iPhoto without having to know these things, but a solid foundation in imaging essentials will help you get more out of iPhoto, your digital camera, and other imaging hardware.

There are a few key points to take away from this little lesson. First, although iPhoto works beautifully with digital cameras, it can also accept images that you've scanned or received from a photofinisher.

Second, those images must be in JPEG format. iPhoto will often accept images in other formats, but the program is designed to work with JPEG images.

And finally, the concept of resolution will arise again and again in your digital imaging endeavors. You'll want big, high-resolution images for good-quality prints, and small, low-resolution images for convenient emailing to friends and family. As described on pages 74 and 96, you can use iPhoto to create low-resolution versions of your images.

## Where Digital Images Come From

iPhoto can work with digital images from a variety of sources.

### Digital camera

Digital cameras are more plentiful and capable than ever. The key factor that differentiates cameras is *resolution*: how many *pixels* of information they store in each image. Entry-level cameras typically provide two-megapixel resolution; you can get a good-quality 8- by 10-inch print from an uncropped two-megapixel image.

Most digital cameras connect to the Mac's USB port. Images are usually stored on removable-media cards; you can also transfer images into iPhoto by connecting a *media reader* to the Mac and inserting the memory card into the reader.

### Scanner

With a scanner, you can create digital images from photographs and other hard-copy originals.

Scanners also connect via USB, although some high-end models connect via FireWire. You'll save your scanned images in JPEG format, and then add them to iPhoto by dragging their icons into the iPhoto window.

For tips on getting high-quality scans, visit www.scantips.com.

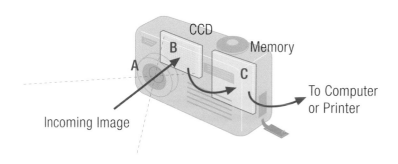

Incoming Image — CCD — B — A — C — Memory — To Computer or Printer

In a digital camera, the image is focused by the lens (**A**) onto the CCD (**B**), where tiny, light-sensitive diodes called photosites convert photons into electrons. Those electrical values are converted into digital data and stored by a memory card or other medium (**C**), from which they can be transferred to a computer or printer.

## Compact disc

For an extra charge, most photofinishers will burn your images on a compact disc in Kodak Picture CD format. You get not only prints and negatives, but also a CD that you use with the Mac.

To learn more about Picture CD, go to www.kodak.com and search for *picture cd*.

## Internet

Many photofinishers also provide extra-cost Internet delivery options. After processing and scanning your film, they send you an email containing a Web address where you can view and download images. After downloading images, you can drag their icons into iPhoto's window.

# A Short Glossary of Imaging Terms

**artifacts** Visible flaws in an image, often as a result of excessive *compression* or when you try to create a large print from a low-resolution image.

**CompactFlash** A removable-memory storage medium commonly used by digital cameras. A CompactFlash card measures 43 by 36 by 3.3 mm. The thicker *Type 2* cards are 5.5 mm wide.

**compression** The process of making image files use less storage space, usually by removing information that our eyes don't detect anyway. The most common form of image compression is *JPEG*.

**EXIF** Pronounced *ex-if*, a standard file format used by virtually all of today's digital cameras. EXIF files use JPEG compression but also contain

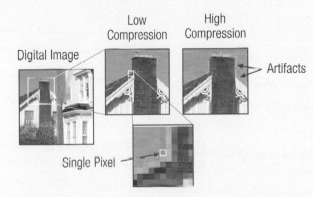

Digital Image | Low Compression | High Compression | Artifacts | Single Pixel

details about each image: the date and time it was taken, its resolution, the type of camera used, the exposure settings, and more. iPhoto retrieves and stores EXIF information when you import images. EXIF stands for *Exchangeable Image File*.

**JPEG** Pronounced *jay-peg*, the most common format for storing digital camera images, and the format that iPhoto is designed to use. Like MP3, JPEG is a *lossy* compression format: it shrinks files by discarding information that we can't perceive anyway. And as with MP3, there are varying degrees of JPEG compression; many imaging programs enable you to specify how heavily JPEG images are compressed. Note that a heavily compressed JPEG image can contain *artifacts*. JPEG stands for *Joint Photographic Experts Group*.

**megapixel** One million pixels.

**pixel** Short for *picture element*, the smallest building block of an image. The number of pixels that a camera or scanner captures determines the *resolution* of the image.

**resolution** **1.** The size of an image, expressed in pixels. For example, an image whose resolution is 640 by 480 contains 480 vertical rows of pixels, each containing 640 pixels from left to right. Common resolutions for digital camera images are 640 by 480, 1280 by 960, 1600 by 1200, 2048 by 1536, and 2272 by 1704.
**2.** A measure of the capabilities of a digital camera or scanner.

**SmartMedia** A commonly used design for removable-memory storage cards. SmartMedia cards measure 45 by 37 by .76 mm.

# Importing Photos into iPhoto

The first step in assembling a digital photo library is to import photos into iPhoto.

iPhoto can directly import photos from many digital cameras. (See a list at www.apple.com/iphoto/compatibility/.) You can specify that iPhoto delete the images from the camera after importing them.

You can also import photos by dragging them from the Finder into the iPhoto window, or by using the Import command in the File menu. You might take this approach if you have scanned JPEG images on your hard drive or if you're using a media reader.

Each time you import images, iPhoto creates a new roll (as in roll of film— get it?). Even when you import just one image, iPhoto creates a roll for it.

After you've finished importing images, you can disconnect your camera. Before you do, however, check to see if its icon appears on your Finder desktop. If its icon does appear, drag it to the Trash or select it and press ⌘-E before disconnecting the camera.

## Importing from a Camera

First, connect your camera to one of your Mac's USB ports (the port on the keyboard is particularly convenient) and turn the camera on.

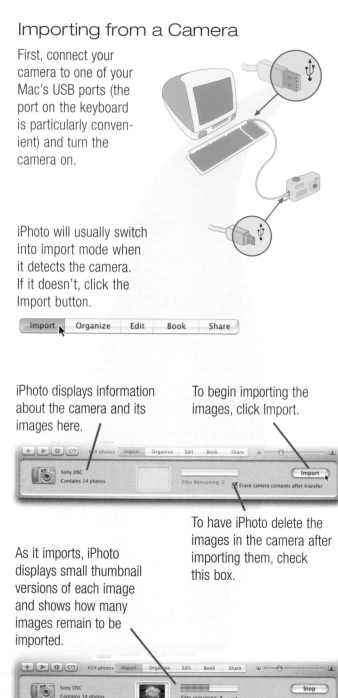

iPhoto will usually switch into import mode when it detects the camera. If it doesn't, click the Import button.

| Import | Organize | Edit | Book | Share |
| --- | --- | --- | --- | --- |

iPhoto displays information about the camera and its images here.

To begin importing the images, click Import.

To have iPhoto delete the images in the camera after importing them, check this box.

As it imports, iPhoto displays small thumbnail versions of each image and shows how many images remain to be imported.

See the process of importing images from a digital camera and from the Finder ⊙ 23–24.

## Importing from the Finder

To import an entire folder full of images, simply drag the folder into the iPhoto window.

iPhoto gives the new roll the same name as the folder that its images came from. You can rename the roll using the technique on page 61.

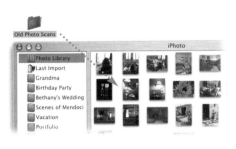

To import only some images, select their icons and then drag them into the iPhoto window.

## Importing from PhotoCDs and Picture CDs

iPhoto can also import images saved on a Kodak PhotoCD or Picture CD. (PhotoCD is an older format that you aren't likely to see too often. Picture CD is a newer format that most photo-finishers use.)

With a PhotoCD, you can't simply drag images from the CD into iPhoto's window. Instead, switch iPhoto into Import mode, insert the CD, and then click the Import button in the bottom-right corner of the iPhoto window.

For a Picture CD, choose Import from iPhoto's File menu, locate the Picture CD, and then locate and double-click the folder named Pictures. Finally, click the Open button. Or, use the Finder to open the Pictures folder on the CD and then drag images into iPhoto's window.

## Where iPhoto Stores Your Photos

When you import photos, iPhoto stores them in a folder called iPhoto Library, located inside the Pictures folder.

Get in the habit of backing up the iPhoto Library Folder frequently to avoid losing your images to a hardware or software problem. And whatever you do, don't futz with the files inside this folder—renaming or moving them could cause iPhoto to have problems finding your photos.

When you import images that are already stored on your hard drive, iPhoto makes duplicate copies of them in your iPhoto Library folder. To avoid wasting disk space, you might want to delete the original files after importing them into iPhoto.

You can store your iPhoto Library folder elsewhere, such

as on an external hard drive, but you must perform a couple of extra steps. First, drag the folder to the desired location, then select it and choose Make Alias from the Finder's File menu. Next, delete the iPhoto Library folder from your Pictures folder, and drag the alias you created to your Pictures folder. Finally, change the name of the alias to *iPhoto Library*.

# After the Import: Getting Organized

iPhoto forces some organization on you by storing each set of imported images as a separate roll. Even if you never use iPhoto's other organizational features, you're still ahead of the old shoebox photo-filing system: you will always be able to view your photos in chronological order.

But don't stop there. Take the time to use at least some of iPhoto's other organizational aids, which let you give titles to rolls and individual images, and assign comments and keywords to images to make them easier to find.

Titles are names or brief descriptions that you assign to photos and rolls: Party Photos, Mary at the Beach, and so on. iPhoto can use these titles as captions for its Web photo albums and books. You can also have iPhoto display titles below each thumbnail image.

Keywords are labels useful for categorizing and locating all the photos of a given kind: vacation shots, baby pictures, mug shots, you name it.

Take advantage of iPhoto's filing features, and you'll be able locate images in, well, a flash.

## Assigning Titles to Images

To assign a title to an image, select the image and type a name in the Title box.

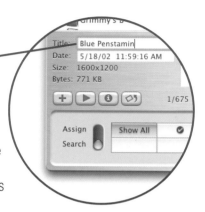

With the Set Title To command in the Edit menu, you can also have iPhoto assign titles to one or more photos for you. iPhoto can use an image's file name, timestamp, or roll name as a title.

## Assigning Comments

You can also assign a comment to a photo; think of a comment as the text you'd normally write on the back of a photograph. You can search for photos based on comments, and iPhoto can use comments as captions for the photos in a book.

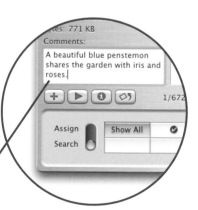

To display the Comments box, click the ⓘ button.

To assign a comment, select the photo and type the comment in the Comments box.

See how to rotate ⊙ 26
and title images ⊙ 29.

## Assigning Titles to Rolls

iPhoto gives a newly imported roll a bland name consisting of a number and the date you imported its images. Use the Title box to give rolls names that are more descriptive.

To title a roll, select it by clicking on its name, then type a title in the Title box.

You can also edit the date of a roll or a single image. This is handy if your digital camera's built-in clock wasn't set correctly or if you want a roll's date to reflect the day you shot its images, not the day you imported them.

After importing images, rotate photos shot in vertical orientation. Select the photo or photos and then click the rotate button (⊙) or press ⌘-R (to rotate counterclockwise) or ⌘-Shift-R (to rotate clockwise).

iPhoto displays rolls chronologically, with the oldest roll at the top of the window. To have your newest rolls appear at the top, choose Preferences from the iPhoto menu and click the Most Recent at Top check box.

And don't forget, you can collapse rolls to hide their images: click on the down-pointing triangle next to the roll's name. Scrolling and changing the size of thumbnails are faster when iPhoto has fewer images to display.

# Assigning and Editing Keywords

Chances are that many of your photos fall into specific categories: baby photos, scenic shots, and so on. By creating and assigning keywords, you make related images easier to find.

For details on searching for keywords and comments, see "Searching for Photos" on page 70.

iPhoto has five predefined keywords that cover common categories. But there's room for another nine, and you can replace the existing ones.

## Assigning Keywords

Assigning a keyword involves selecting one or more images, and then clicking the desired keyword or keywords.

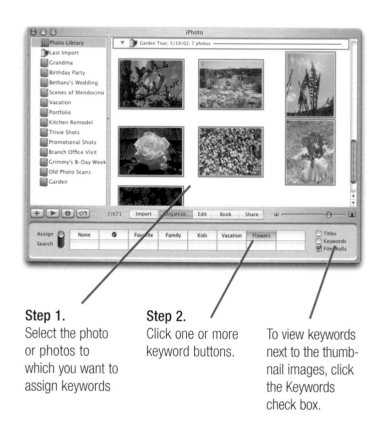

**Step 1.**
Select the photo or photos to which you want to assign keywords

**Step 2.**
Click one or more keyword buttons.

To view keywords next to the thumbnail images, click the Keywords check box.

## Editing Keywords

To edit keywords, choose Edit Keywords from the Edit menu or press ⌘-K.

When you've finished editing keywords, click Done.

You can't edit the checkmark keyword, which you might use to mark images you want to print, edit, or work with in other ways.

To create a new keyword, click in a blank keyword box and type the keyword. To edit an existing keyword, select it and type a new keyword.

### Edit Keywords Carefully

If you've already assigned a given keyword to some photos, think twice about changing that keyword. If you do change it, the photos to which you've assigned the keyword will inherit the new keyword.

For example, say you've assigned a Friends keyword to photos of all your friends. If you later edit the Friends keyword to Enemies, all the photos of your friends will take on the new keyword.

# Creating Albums

Getting photos back from a lab is always exciting, but what's really fun is creating a photo album that turns a collection of photos into a story.

An iPhoto album contains a series of photographs sequenced in an order that helps tell a story or document an event.

Creating albums in iPhoto is a simple matter of dragging thumbnail images. You can add and remove photos to and from albums at any time, and you can sequence the photos in whatever order you like. You can even include the same photo in many different albums.

The photos in an album might be from one roll, or from a dozen different rolls. Just as an iTunes playlist lets you create your own music compilations, an iPhoto album lets you create your own image compilations.

And once you create albums, you can share them in a variety of ways.

## Step 1: Create an Empty Album

To create a new album, choose New Album from the File menu or click the Add Album button (⊕).

## Step 2: Name the Album

iPhoto asks you to name the new album.

## Step 3: Add Photos

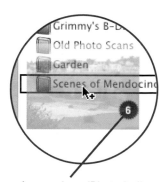

As you drag, iPhoto indicates how many photos you've selected.

After you've named the album, begin dragging photos into it. You can drag photos one at a time, or select multiple photos and drag them in all at once.

See techniques and shortcuts for creating and working with albums and selecting photos ⊙ **27-28**.

## A Shortcut for Creating Albums

You can create an album and add images to it in one step. Select one or more images and drag them to a blank spot of the Photo Library list area. iPhoto creates a new album and adds the photos to it.

When you use this technique, iPhoto gives the new album a generic name, such as *Album-1*. To rename the album, double-click its name and type a new name.

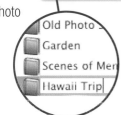

## Tips for Selecting Photos

Selecting photos is a common activity in iPhoto: you select photos in order to delete them, add them to an album, move them around within an album, and more.

When working with multiple photos, remember the standard Mac OS selection shortcuts: To select a range of photos, click on the first one and Shift-click on the last one. To select multiple photos that aren't adjacent to each other, press ⌘ while clicking on each photo.

## Organizing an Album

The order of the photos in an album is important: when you create slide shows, books, or Web photo galleries, iPhoto presents the photos in the order in which they appear in the album.

Once you've created an album, you may want to fine-tune the order of its photos.

To edit an album, click on its name.

You can also assign keywords, titles, and comments to photos while working in an album.

To change the order of the photos, drag them. Here, the flower close-up is being moved so it will appear after the other two garden shots.

Don't want a photo in an album after all? Select it and press the Delete key. This removes the photo from the album, but not from your hard drive or Photo Library

# Editing Photos

Many photos can benefit from some tweaking. Maybe you'd like to crop out that huge telephone pole that distracts from your subject. Maybe the exposure is too light, too dark, or lacks contrast. Or maybe the camera's flash gave your subject's eyes the dreaded red-eye flaw.

iPhoto's edit mode can fix these problems. And it does so in a clever way that doesn't replace your original image: if you don't like your edits, choose Revert to Original from the File menu.

iPhoto isn't a full-fledged digital darkroom—you can't, for example, retouch a photo to remove a scratch. For tasks like these, you'll want a separate image-editing program, such as Adobe Photoshop. But iPhoto's editing features address many common image problems. And if you have a separate image-editing program, you can set up iPhoto to work along with it.

## Editing Essentials

To switch to iPhoto's edit mode, select a photo—either in the iPhoto Library or in an album—and click the Edit button. Or, simply double-click the photo.

Cropping controls; see "Cropping Photos," on the next page.

Use the size slider to zoom in and out. When zoomed in, you can quickly scroll by pressing ⌘-spacebar and then dragging within the image.

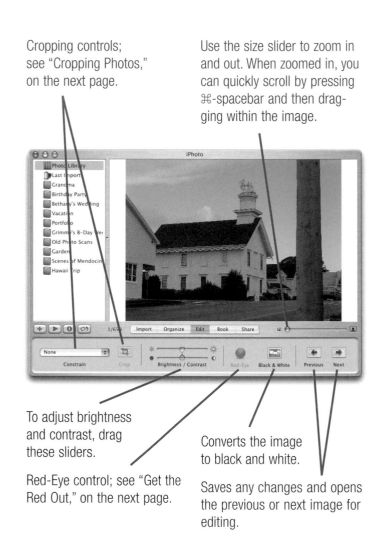

To adjust brightness and contrast, drag these sliders.

Red-Eye control; see "Get the Red Out," on the next page.

Converts the image to black and white.

Saves any changes and opens the previous or next image for editing.

See techniques for cropping images  **31**
and tips for iPhoto's image edit mode ◉ **32**.

## Cropping Photos

To crop out unwanted portions of a photo, first click and drag within the image to indicate which portion you want to retain.

Drag to create a selection. To move the selection, drag within it. To resize it, drag any corner. To deselect the area, click on the image anywhere outside the selection.

If you have a specific output destination in mind for the photo, choose the most appropriate option from the Constrain pop-up menu. For example, if you plan to print a vertically oriented 5 by 7 photo, choose 5 x 7 Portrait. iPhoto restricts the proportions of the cropping area to match the option you choose. To create a cropping selection of any size, choose None.

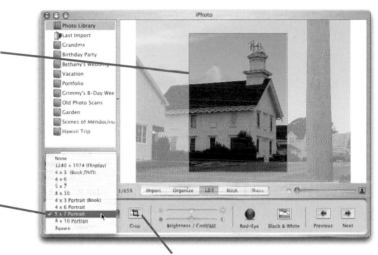

To apply the crop area to the image, click Crop.

## Get the Red Out

Red-eye is a common problem caused by the bright light of an electronic flash reflecting off a subject's retinas and the blood vessels around them.

Be sure the Constrain pop-up menu is set to None, then drag to select the subject's eyes.

To apply the fix, click the Red-Eye button.

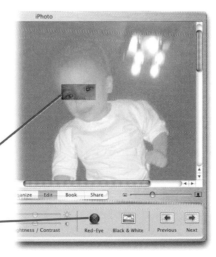
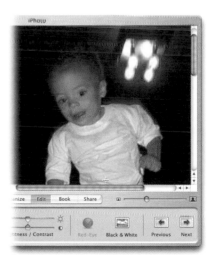

# Using the Edit Window

Normally, iPhoto displays the image you're editing within the iPhoto window itself. But iPhoto also provides a separate edit window that you may prefer. One reason to use an edit window is that you can have multiple edit windows open simultaneously, enabling you to compare images. And the edit window has some features that the edit pane lacks.

## Displaying the Edit Window

To open an image in a separate window, press the Option key while double-clicking on the image. You can also use the Preferences command to have iPhoto always use the separate window when you double-click on an image.

Enlarges or reduces the image to fit the size of the edit window.

To customize the edit window toolbar, click Customize.

You can enter a custom constrain dimension here.

Zoom in and out. When zoomed in, you can quickly scroll by pressing ⌘-spacebar and dragging within the image.

Do you frequently crop to specific constraints? Customize the toolbar and add those cropping constraints for one-click access.

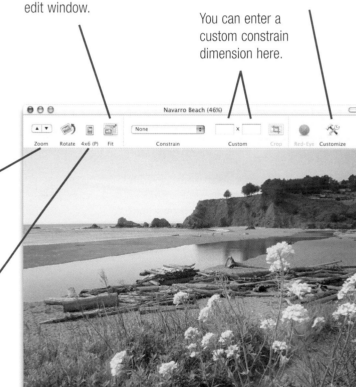

See how to display and
use iPhoto's edit window ⊙ **32**.

## Using iPhoto with Other Imaging Programs

If you have Adobe Photoshop or another image editing program, you might want to set up iPhoto to work with it: when you double-click an image in iPhoto's Organize view, your Mac will switch to your image editing program, which will open the image.

Choose Preferences from the iPhoto menu, and in the area labeled Double-Clicking Photos Opens Them In, click the Other button. Next, locate and double-click your image editing program.

## Restoring the Original Image

iPhoto also includes iSafetyNet. Actually, there is no feature by that name, but there might as well be: even after you've cropped and otherwise modified an image, you can always revert to the original version by selecting the image and then choosing Revert to Original from the File menu.

## Customizing the Edit Window Toolbar

To customize the edit window toolbar, click its Customize button or choose Customize Toolbar from the Window menu.

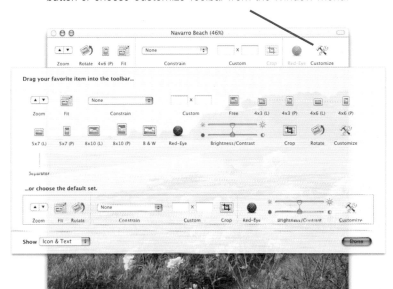

You can then add and remove tools to suit your needs.

To add a tool, drag it to the toolbar. To remove a tool you don't use, drag it off of the toolbar.

You can also rearrange tools by dragging them left and right on the toolbar. And using the Show pop-up menu, you can specify whether the toolbar appears with icons and text, with just icons, or with just text.

# Searching for Photos

If you've taken the time to assign titles, comments, and keywords to your photos, here's where your investment pays off.

You can use iPhoto's search feature to locate photos that match a certain keyword or combination of keywords. And, if you use the Preferences command to switch to iPhoto's text-search mode, you can also search for text contained in a photo's comment, title, file name, or keyword.

To search in iPhoto, you must be in Organize mode. If you're in a different mode, click the Organize button. iPhoto displays the keywords at the bottom of its window.

When you search for photos in your library, iPhoto displays only those photos that meet your criteria. If a photo is contained in a roll that you've collapsed (by clicking the triangle next to the roll's name), iPhoto displays only the roll name. You'll need to expand the roll to see the found photos inside.

## Searching by Keywords

**Step 1.**
To begin a search, click the Organize pane's switch to the Search position.

**Step 2.**
Click the keyword you want to search for. You can further narrow your search by clicking on another keyword— for example, clicking Vacation to find all photos of flowers taken on a vacation. To widen the search, click on a highlighted keyword again to deselect it.

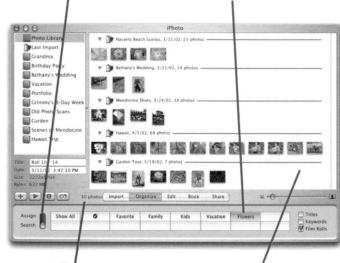

iPhoto displays the number of photos it found.

iPhoto displays only those photos that have the search keyword or keywords assigned to them. To display all photos again, click the Show All button in the Organize pane.

## Searching for Text

iPhoto's text-search mode is particularly powerful. It lets you search for photos based on text in titles, comments, file names, and keywords. Building on the previous example, if I typed *flowers* in the text-search box, iPhoto would find all photos with Flowers as their keyword.

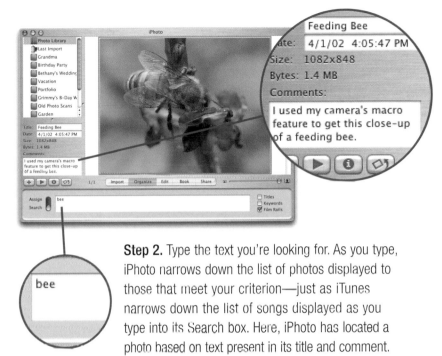

**Step 1.** To search for text, you must tweak one of iPhoto's Preferences settings. In the area of the Preferences dialog box labeled Assign/Search Uses, click the Comments button. The Organize pane changes as shown here.

**Step 2.** Type the text you're looking for. As you type, iPhoto narrows down the list of photos displayed to those that meet your criterion—just as iTunes narrows down the list of songs displayed as you type into its Search box. Here, iPhoto has located a photo based on text present in its title and comment.

## EXIF Exposed: Getting Information About Photos

I mentioned earlier that digital cameras store information along with each photo—the date and time when the photo was taken, its exposure, the kind of camera used, and more. This is called the EXIF data.

iPhoto saves this EXIF data when you import photos. To view it, select a photo and choose Show Info from the File menu (⌘-I).

Much of this information may not be useful to you, but some of it might. If you have more than one digital cam- era, for example, you can use the window's Photo tab to see which camera you used for a given shot.

If you're interested in learning more about the nuts and bolts of photography, explore the Exposure tab to see what kinds of exposure settings your camera used.

At the very least, you might just want to explore the Photo Info window to see the kind of information iPhoto is keeping track of for you.

# Sharing Photos on a HomePage

Everyone likes to get photos in the mail. Email, however, is another story. Too many people make the mistake of emailing massive image files that take forever to transfer, and end up bogging down their recipients' email sessions.

And because dealing with email attachments is frequently a hassle—particularly when you're emailing from a Mac to a Windows computer, or vice versa—there's a good chance the recipients will never see the images anyway.

A better way to share photos is to publish them on a Web site, specifically on an Apple HomePage. iPhoto works together with Apple's free iTools service to make Web photo albums easy to create—it takes only a couple of mouse clicks to make your images available to a global audience. You can also password-protect albums so only certain people can see them.

Note that you must have an Apple iTools account to create a HomePage. To register for a free account, go to www.apple.com/itools.

## Creating a HomePage

You can create a HomePage containing just one photo, a selection of photos, or an entire album. You don't even have to create an album to create a HomePage—you can select some images in the Photo Library and proceed directly to the HomePage button. But it's smarter to create an album, so you can control the order in which the photos appear on the HomePage.

Regardless of where your HomePage originates, you must click the Share button in the iPhoto window before you can publish your photos on the Web.

Organize the album's photos in the order you want them to appear. To publish only a few photos, select them first.

To begin the publishing process, be sure you're connected to the Internet, then click the HomePage button.

See how to create a Web photo album ⊙ 35;
view this album at http://homepage.mac.com/jimheid.

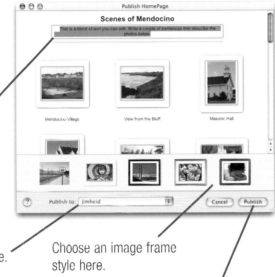

iPhoto connects with Apple's iTools service and, after a few moments, displays a preview of your HomePage.

iPhoto uses the album name for the name of the HomePage, and uses the title you assigned to each photo as its caption. You can edit any text item in the HomePage preview.

Be sure your iTools account name appears here.

Choose an image frame style here.

When you've finished previewing the HomePage, click Publish to transfer the images to iTools.

After iPhoto has transferred your photos, a dialog box displays the address of your new HomePage.

You can copy this address to the Mac's Clipboard by dragging across it, then pressing ⌘-C. Paste the address into an email message to notify people that you've published the album.

To see the new HomePage album, click Visit Page Now.

## Editing a HomePage Album

What if you publish a HomePage album and then realize that you want to make changes? Sorry, no can do—at least not in iPhoto. But you can edit a HomePage album by going to Apple's iTools site, logging in, and then using the iTools editing features.

With the Home-Page's iTools page, you can edit albums you've published and create several other kinds of Web pages.

One of the changes you can make is to choose from a wider variety of themes (such as Birthday, Spring, and Halloween) and styles than iPhoto provides. You can also put a page counter on your HomePage album to see how many times it's viewed.

# More Internet Sharing Options

## Emailing Photos

Even after my earlier rant, I'll be the first to admit that email is the easiest way to share just a few photos with someone over the Internet—especially if you take advantage of iPhoto's ability to make images smaller for faster transfers.

### Step 1:
### Select the Photos

Select the images you want to email...

...and then click the Mail button.

### Step 2:
### Reduce Their Size

iPhoto can make the images smaller before emailing. (This doesn't change the dimensions or file size of your original images, which iPhoto always stores in all their high-resolution glory.)

iPhoto estimates the size of the final attachments. If you're sending images to someone who is connecting using a modem (as opposed to a high-speed connection), try to keep the estimated size below 300KB or so. As a rule of thumb: each 100KB will take about 15 seconds to transfer over a 56 kbps modem.

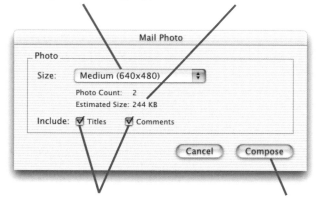

You have the option to include titles and comments along with the images—another good reason to assign this information when organizing your photos.

After you've specified mail settings, click Compose.

After iPhoto creates smaller versions of photos, it starts the Mac OS X Mail program. Your photos are added to a new email, which you can complete and send on its way.

# Exporting Web Albums and Mailing with Entourage

## Exporting a Web Page

You can also export photos and albums as a Web page to post on sites other than an Apple HomePage. iPhoto creates small thumbnail versions of your Images as well as the HTML pages that display them. (HTML stands for Hyper-Text Markup Language—it's the set of codes used to design Web pages.)

If you're a Web publisher, you can modify these pages as you see fit, and then upload them to a Web site.

To export a Web page, select some photos or an album, click iPhoto's Export button (or press ⌘-E), then click the Web Page tab.

Specify the page appearance and dimensions of the thumbnails and the images, then click Export. It's a good idea to create a new folder for the Web page; iPhoto will create several folders and pages within it.

## A Better HTML Export

iPhoto's Export command yields a rather bland-looking photo album. You can spice up iPhoto's HTML export feature by installing Simeon Leifer's free BetterHTMLExport, available from software download sites. BetterHTMLExport provides numerous design templates for you to choose from and modify.

## Burning HTML Albums on a CD

Even if you aren't a Web jockey, there's a good reason to consider exporting an album as a set of Web pages: you can burn the exported pages onto CDs, and then mail them to others. They'll be able to view the album on their Macs or PCs using a Web browser—no attachment hassles, no long downloads.

After exporting the Web page, copy its folders and HTML pages to a blank CD-R disc. Burn the disc, eject it, and you have a photo Web site on a disc.

To view the site, simply double-click on the file named Index.html. You might be tempted to rename that file to something a bit more friendly, such as open_me.html, but resist the urge. If you change the name, the links in the Web album won't work. Similarly, don't rename any image files or move them from their folders.

## Mailing with Microsoft Entourage

You don't use Mac OS X's email program? Me neither—I prefer Microsoft Entourage X. Thanks to Simon Jacquier's iPhoto Entourage Patcher, those of us who use Entourage X can take advantage of iPhoto's emailing features, too. This free program alters iPhoto to use Entourage X instead of Mail It works like a charm.

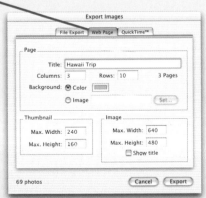

# Printing Photos and Ordering Prints

Internet photo sharing is great, but hard copy isn't dead. You might want to share photos with people who don't have computers. Or, you might want to tack a photo to a bulletin board or hang it on your wall—you'll never see "suitable for framing" stamped on an email message.

iPhoto makes hard copy easy. If you have a photo-inkjet printer, you can use iPhoto to create beautiful color prints in a variety of sizes. This assumes, of course, that your photos are both beautiful and in color.

Another option is iPhoto's print-ordering features, which let you order photographic prints in sizes ranging from 4 by 6 inches to 20 by 30 inches.

Printing with iPhoto is straightforward, but to get the best results, you'll want to use images with a resolution high enough to yield sharp results at your chosen print size.

## Printing Your Photos

iPhoto works well with today's photo-inkjet printers and lets you create prints in several sizes and formats.

To print just one photo, select it and then choose Print from the File menu (⌘-P). To print multiple photos, select them before choosing Print.

Be sure your printer is selected here.

iPhoto includes preset printing options for many popular inkjet printers. Choose the preset that best matches the type of paper you're using.

Use the Standard Prints style to create prints in common sizes. Other style options are Contact Sheet, Full Page, and Greeting Card.

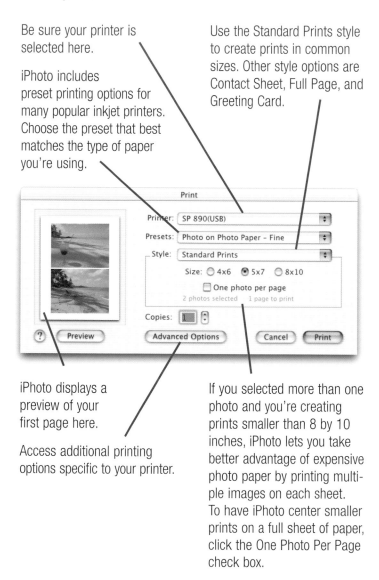

iPhoto displays a preview of your first page here.

Access additional printing options specific to your printer.

If you selected more than one photo and you're creating prints smaller than 8 by 10 inches, iPhoto lets you take better advantage of expensive photo paper by printing multiple images on each sheet. To have iPhoto center smaller prints on a full sheet of paper, click the One Photo Per Page check box.

See the print-ordering process ⊚ **36**,
a photo printer ⊚ **40**,
and some fun output options ⊚ **42**.

## Ordering Prints

To order prints, first select the photos you want prints of, then click the Order Prints button in iPhoto's Share pane.

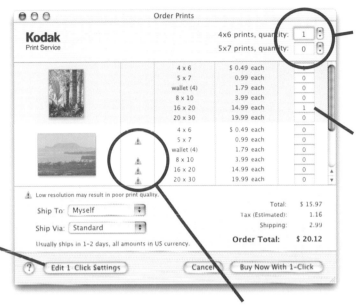

Want a 4 by 6 or 5 by 7 of every photo? Type the quantity here.

Specify how many prints you want for each size.

To order prints, you must first set up an Apple ID account and enable 1-Click ordering. For instructions, click the help icon next to this button.

Low-resolution images may yield poor prints at larger sizes; see the sidebar below for details.

## Resolution's Relationship to Print Quality

If you're working with low-resolution images—ones taken with a digital camera at its low-resolution setting, for example—you may see iPhoto's dreaded low-resolution warning icon when printing, ordering prints, or creating a book.

This is iPhoto's way ⚠ of telling you that an image

doesn't have enough pixels—enough digital information—to yield a good-quality print at the size that you've chosen.

Don't feel obligated to cancel a print job or an order if you see this warning. I've ordered books containing low-resolution images and they still look beautiful.

Yes, some artifacts are visible at times, but I'd rather have a memorable book with some flawed photos than no book at all.

The table here lists the minimum resolution an image should have to yield a good print at various sizes.

### Print Sizes and Resolution

| For This Print Size (Inches) | Image Resolution Should be at Least (Pixels) |
|---|---|
| Wallet | 320 by 240 |
| 4 by 6 | 640 by 480 |
| 5 by 7 | 1024 by 768 |
| 8 by 10 | 1536 by 1024 |
| 16 by 20 or larger | 1600 by 1200 |

# Creating Books

With iPhoto's Book button and Apple's help, you can turn an album of photos into a hard-bound, linen-covered book. iPhoto books make spectacular gifts and are ideal for promotional portfolios and other business applications, too.

To create a book, first create an album containing the photos you want to publish, in the order you want them to appear. Then, click iPhoto's Book button to display the Book pane.

Next, choose a theme design from the Theme pop-up menu. Finally, arrange the photos and text captions on each page as described here.

One last note: Because of the printing method used to create iPhoto books, Apple recommends against including black-and-white photos in a book.

## Browsing Books

iPhoto provides a variety of book designs, called *themes*.

### Catalog

Places up to eight photos on a page, with room for captions and descriptions.

### Classic

Symmetrical page designs with up to four photos per page, with captions in the elegant Baskerville typeface.

### Picture Book

Positions photos as bleeds—the photos extend to the edges of the page.

### Portfolio

Allows up to four photos per page and provides for captions and titles.

### Story Book

Positions photos askew on the page and leaves room for storytelling.

### Year Book

Allows for up to 32 photos per page— ideal for a class yearbook or a collection of police mug shots.

See an iPhoto book ◉ 41.

## Designing a Book

You design a book one page at a time. iPhoto displays a thumbnail version of the current page; to zoom in on the thumbnail, use the size slider. You can edit the text on each page and choose a different design from the Page Design pop-up menu.

Each theme has a variety of page designs; choose a design here. Some designs place more photos on each page than others.

**Tips:** To apply a page design to all subsequent pages in the book, press the Option key while choosing the design. And if you're working with low-resolution images, use a design that puts several images on a page. Each image will be smaller, and thus more likely to print with acceptable quality.

To work on a different page, select it. To move a page within the book, drag it left or right.

**Note:** Moving a page also changes the order of the photos In your album.

The Portfolio theme is my favorite; I like its contemporary, elegant look.

To hide the faint lines that iPhoto draws on-screen around title and comment boxes, uncheck this box. Either way, these lines will not print.

You can include titles, comments, and page numbers in your book.

**Tip:** You can change the formatting of these items by selecting the text you want to change, and then using the Font command in the Edit menu.

When you change the number of photos on a page, iPhoto changes the placement of all photos on subsequent pages. To ensure that the photos on the page you're working on will remain on that page, click Lock Page.

To preview the book, click Preview. You can also use the book preview window to edit captions.

# Creating Slide Shows

iPhoto's printing and Internet-sharing features are enough to ensure that a photo need never lead a life of obscurity.

But iPhoto doesn't stop there. It also lets you display photos as an on-screen slide show, complete with background music.

iPhoto's slide show feature displays a series of photos on your screen, with a lovely cross-dissolve effect—one photo fades out as the next one fades in.

## Viewing a Slide Show

Most of the time, you'll want to add photos to an album before viewing them as a slide show. That way, you can arrange the photos in a sequence that best tells your story.

But, when you're after immediate gratification—if you want to screen a roll of images immediately after importing them, for example—you can view a slide show from a series of images you've selected in the Photo Library.

No matter what mode iPhoto is in, a slide show is one click away: Just click the Play button (▶), which appears below the Photo Library list.

## Slide Show Keyboard Controls

To pause a slide show, press the spacebar. If the slide show has music, the music will continue to play but the images won't change. To resume the slide show, press the spacebar again.

To adjust the speed of the slide show, use the up and down arrow keys. To manually move through the slide show, use the left and right arrow keys.

## Videotaping a Slide Show

Many PowerBooks have S-video jacks that enable you to display their screen images on a TV set or record them using a camcorder or videocassette recorder. You can take advantage of these TV-savvy Macs to record a slide show on tape.

First, connect the PowerBook's S-video connector to a camcorder or VCR, and then open System Preferences and use Displays to turn on video mirroring.

Next, press your video deck's Record button, and begin playing back the slide show.

To record the background music, too, connect the Mac's speaker jack to your video deck's audio-input jacks.

Watch an iPhoto slide show
come together ⊙ 33.

# Customizing the Slide Show

When you start a slide show using the Play button, iPhoto displays each image for two seconds as it plays a music soundtrack.

You can specify how long the images display and tell iPhoto to play back a different music file, including one from your iTunes library. To do so, use iPhoto's Preferences command, or click the Slide Show button in the Share pane to display the Slide Show Settings dialog box.

Type a duration for each image or click the up and down arrows to set a duration.

When this box is checked, iPhoto will repeat the slide show until time itself comes to an end or until you press the Esc key or the mouse button, whichever comes first.

To choose a different song, choose Other from the Music pop-up menu, then navigate to your iTunes Music folder and double-click on the desired tune.

When you select a new song for a slide show, iPhoto makes that song the default. Each time you start a slide show by clicking the Play button, iPhoto will play the last song you selected. To specify a different song, return to the Share pane, click the Slide Show button, and choose a different option from the Music pop-up menu. You can also use the Preferences dialog box to change the default song.

# Cleaning Up the Music Menu

Each time you choose a new song, iPhoto adds the song to its Music pop-up menu. Over time, the menu can become cluttered. To clean it up and remove songs you aren't planning to use again, choose

Edit List from the Music pop-up menu, and then delete the songs you don't want to be listed in the menu. (The songs won't be deleted from the iTunes Music folder or your hard drive.)

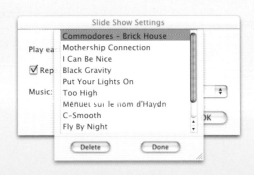

# More Ways to Share Photos

You can export a series of images in QuickTime movie format, again adding a music soundtrack if you like. You can publish the resulting movie on a Web site, burn it to a CD, or bring it into iDVD and burn it to a DVD.

Looking for still more ways to share? Redecorate your Macintosh desktop with your favorite photo. Or, use a set of photos as a screen saver. iPhoto makes it easy to do both.

It's obvious: If your digital photos aren't getting seen, it isn't iPhoto's fault.

## Exporting Photos as Movies

Why export still images in a movie format? Because iPhoto will add a music soundtrack and cross-dissolves between images. Think of an iPhoto QuickTime movie as a portable slide show. Email it, post it on a Web site, or burn it to a CD or DVD—it will play back on any Mac or Windows computer that has QuickTime installed.

Portable slide show: An iPhoto-created QuickTime movie playing back in the QuickTime Player program.

You can import an iPhoto-created QuickTime movie into iDVD and burn it to a DVD disc. In fact, given that iDVD's slide show feature lacks a cross-dissolve effect, you might prefer to use iPhoto QuickTime movies to present photos on DVDs. However, further proving that life is a game of trade-offs, iPhoto lacks iDVD's ability to time a slide show to a piece of music. In an iPhoto QuickTime movie, the music stops abruptly after the last image displays.

To export images as a QuickTime movie, select a set of images or switch to an album. Click the Share button, then click the Export button in the Share pane.

Specify the duration for each image to display.

You can specify that iPhoto add a background color or background image to the movie. The color or image appears whenever the dimensions of the currently displayed photo don't match that of the movie itself. (For example, in a 640 by 480 movie, the background will be visible in photos shot in vertical orientation.) The background will also be visible at the beginning and end of the movie—before the first image fades in and after the last image fades out.

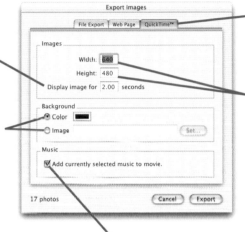

Click the QuickTime tab to access movie-export options.

Specify the desired dimensions for the movie, in pixels. The preset values shown here work well, but if you specify smaller dimensions, such as 320 by 240, you'll get a smaller movie file—useful if you plan to distribute the movie over the Internet.

When this box is checked, iPhoto uses the last song you selected as the soundtrack for the movie. To create a silent movie, uncheck this box.

## Using Photos as Desktop Images and Screen Savers

The Share pane's Desktop and Screen Saver buttons let you share photos with yourself. Select a photo and click Desktop, and iPhoto replaces the Mac's desktop with the image you selected.

With the Screen Saver button, you can use an iPhoto album as fuel for Mac OS X's screen saver. *Warning:* Using vacation photos as a screen saver has been proven to cause wanderlust.

Desktop    Screen Saver

# iPhoto Tips

## Enhancing iPhoto

Several software add-ons can enhance iPhoto. I've already mentioned some of them: the Entourage email patcher, which adapts iPhoto's email-sharing button to work with Microsoft Entourage X, and BetterHTML-Export, which improves on iPhoto's Web-export features.

Let me share a few more add-ons you might want to explore.

## Enhance Those Pixels

Another popular iPhoto supplement is Caffeine Software's PixelNhance. This free utility has excellent brightness, contrast, color-correction, and sharpening controls. Use iPhoto's Preferences command to have PixelNhance open when you double-click a photo for editing, or simply drag photos from iPhoto's window into PixelNhance. PixelNhance's clever before-and-after display makes it easy to assess your tweaks.

## iPhoto Library Manager

You might find that iPhoto's single photo library is too restrictive. Maybe you'd like to have separate libraries for different types of photos. Or, maybe you'd like each member of the family to have his or her own library.

One way to have multiple photo libraries is to take advantage of Mac OS X's ability to support multiple users on one computer. If you create separate users for each person who uses your Mac, iPhoto will create a separate library for each user. (To learn how to create additional user accounts, search for *users* in the Mac's online help.)

But logging in and out of the system is time consuming. Can't you just set up iPhoto to support multiple iPhoto Library folders? With Brian Webster's free iPhoto Library Manager utility, you can. This simple utility lets you create multiple iPhoto libraries and switch among them.

## Apple's iPhoto AppleScripts

iPhoto itself does not use AppleScript—at least not yet—but Apple has developed some free scripts that do useful things. To use one, all you need to do is drag photos from iPhoto onto a script's icon. The Show Image File script is the most useful: drag a photo from iPhoto's window, drop it onto this script, and the Finder will ferret out the photo's original image file and highlight it for you.

*Warning*: As I've already mentioned, you should never rename or move files located within the iPhoto Library folder.

Get the iPhoto AppleScripts at www.apple.com/applescript/iphoto.

## Portraits & Prints

This inexpensive utility from Econ Technologies goes beyond iPhoto's printing features to let you mix and match photos of various sizes on a single sheet of paper. See it in action in chapter 38 of the DVD included with this book. Add the companion Template Maker utility, and you can create your own printing templates.

See software and hardware add-ons
for digital photography ⊚ **38-40**.

## Beyond Prints

Several online photofinishers will print your photos on more than just paper. As you can see in chapter 42 of the DVD, I've had photos printed onto mugs, mouse pads, T-shirts, and even cookies. (And no, the cookies don't really taste like poodle—they're pretty good, despite all the artificial coloring.)

I ordered my photo doodads from ClubPhoto (www.clubphoto. com), but you can also get off-beat output options from Image Edit (www.image-edit.com), Mystic Color Lab (www.mystic-colorlab.com), and Kodak's Picture Center (www.kodak.com).

## Dragging Photos to the Finder

If you drag an image to the Finder desktop or to a folder window, iPhoto makes a duplicate copy of the image file. I use this technique in the iMovie segment of the DVD (chapter 46).

To have iPhoto make an alias (a shortcut) of the image file, press ⌘-Option while dragging the photo to the Finder.

## Copying Images from iPhoto

It's likely that you'll want to include photos in documents you're creating in Microsoft Word or other programs. It's easy: just drag the image from iPhoto into your document.

You can also drag images from iPhoto into iDVD; you can see this in action in the iDVD segment of the DVD (chapter 80).

Plus, you can drag images from iPhoto onto the icons of programs in your Dock or in a Finder window. For example, to open an image in Photoshop, drag the image to Photoshop's icon.

## Removing Without Deleting

You can use drag and drop to remove photos from a roll without deleting them from your hard drive. First, drag the photos to the Finder to make copies of them. Next, delete them from the roll where they appear. Finally, reimport the photos by dragging them back into iPhoto's window, where they'll appear in their own new roll.

## Controlling the Camera Connection

You can use the Image Capture program, included with Mac OS X, to control what happens when you connect a digital camera to your Mac. You can have the Mac start up iPhoto, start up Image Capture or a different program, or do nothing at all.

# More iPhoto Tips

## Duplicating an Album

There may be times when you'll want several versions of an album. For example, you might have one version with photos sequenced for a slide show and another version with photos organized for a book. Or you might simply want to experiment with several different photo arrangements until you find the one you like best.

iPhoto makes this kind of experimentation easy. Simply duplicate an album by selecting its name and choosing Duplicate from the File menu (⌘-D). iPhoto makes a duplicate of the album, which you can rename and experiment with.

You can make as many duplicates of an album as you like.

## Switching Between Search Modes

If you'll be switching between text- and keyword-search modes during a lengthy photo-finding session, don't bother closing iPhoto's Preferences window. Simply leave it open—iPhoto applies new preferences settings the moment you make them.

## The Why and How of Duplicating Photos

You have a photo that appears in multiple albums, but you want to edit its appearance in just one album, leaving the original version unchanged in other albums.

Time for the Duplicate command: select the photo and choose Duplicate from the File menu (⌘-D). Now edit the duplicate.

You can also use the Duplicate command to create special effects for iPhoto's slide show and QuickTime movie features. Make a few duplicates of an image, and modify each duplicate in some way. Sequence each image in an album, and when you play the slide show or QuickTime movie, each version will fade into the next.

## From Import to Album

If you have photos on your Finder desktop—whether on your hard drive, a Picture CD, or a digital camera's memory card—you can import them and create an album in one fell swoop. Simply drag the photos from the Finder into a blank area of the Photo Library list. iPhoto will import the photos, storing them in their own roll. iPhoto will also create an album and add the photos to it.